THREE SHEETS IN THE WIND

THREE SHEETS IN THE WIND

thelwell's

MANUAL OF SAILING

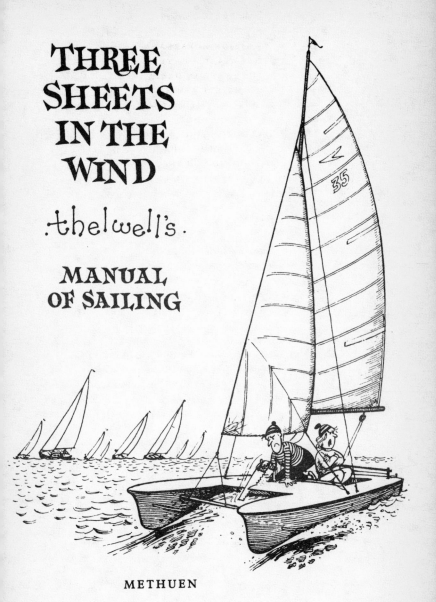

METHUEN

A Methuen Paperback

THREE SHEETS IN THE WIND

ISBN 0 417 01120 2

First published in Great Britain 1973 by Eyre Methuen Ltd
Magnum edition published 1976
Reprinted 1981

Copyright © 1973 by Norman Thelwell

This edition published 1982
Reprinted 1984, 1987
by Methuen London Ltd
11 New Fetter Lane, London EC4P 4EE

Made and printed in Great Britain
by Richard Clay Ltd, Bungay, Suffolk

CONTENTS

GUY ROPE (CAPTAIN)

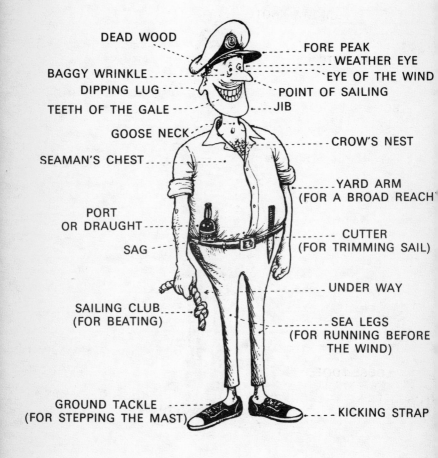

DEAD WOOD

FORE PEAK

WEATHER EYE

BAGGY WRINKLE

EYE OF THE WIND

DIPPING LUG

POINT OF SAILING

TEETH OF THE GALE

JIB

GOOSE NECK

CROW'S NEST

SEAMAN'S CHEST

YARD ARM
(FOR A BROAD REACH)

PORT
OR DRAUGHT

SAG

CUTTER
(FOR TRIMMING SAIL)

UNDER WAY

SAILING CLUB
(FOR BEATING)

SEA LEGS
(FOR RUNNING BEFORE
THE WIND)

GROUND TACKLE
(FOR STEPPING THE MAST)

KICKING STRAP

MAY DAY (FIRST MATE)

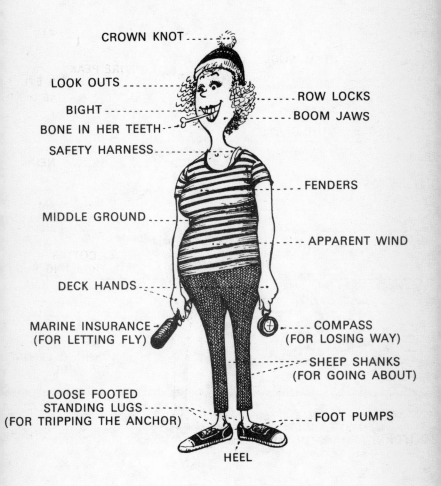

CROWN KNOT

LOOK OUTS

BIGHT

BONE IN HER TEETH

SAFETY HARNESS

ROW LOCKS

BOOM JAWS

FENDERS

MIDDLE GROUND

APPARENT WIND

DECK HANDS

MARINE INSURANCE
(FOR LETTING FLY)

COMPASS
(FOR LOSING WAY)

SHEEP SHANKS
(FOR GOING ABOUT)

LOOSE FOOTED
STANDING LUGS
(FOR TRIPPING THE ANCHOR)

FOOT PUMPS

HEEL

TECHNICAL TERMS

ENTERING UP THE LOG

A SAILOR'S BUNK

A SEA SHANTY

FREE BOARD

CAPSIZE

PERSONAL BUOYANCY

REEF POINTS

FLINDER'S BAR

LASHING DOWN

LOSING WAY

BOOM

A WINDLASS

DRESSED OVERALL

MAKING SAIL

A SAILING HORSE

TIDE RACE

NAVIGATION MARKS

BY AND LARGE

LYING IN THE ROADS

THE PLIMSOLL MARK

"WHERE'S THIS PLACE, MATE?"

THE CALL OF THE SEA

SAILING IS THE FASTEST GROWING PARTICIPATION
SPORT OF MODERN TIMES

IT IS NO LONGER THE EXCLUSIVE PRESERVE
OF THE VERY RICH

NOR DOES ONE HAVE TO BE WEALTHY TO OWN
ONE'S OWN CRAFT

SAILING IS A FAMILY SPORT

THERE IS NO ROOM FOR THE GENERATION GAP
IN A BOAT

WHETHER YOUR PREFERENCE IS FOR THE FEEL OF A CAPRICIOUS
BREEZE IN YOUR CANVAS –

OR FOR THE HEADY EXCITEMENT OF A SURGING POWER BOAT –

WHETHER YOU FIND YOURSELF DRAWN IRRESISTIBLY
TO THE OPEN SEA –

OR TAKE YOUR PLEASURE IN INLAND WATERS . . .

THERE IS NOTHING QUITE LIKE THE THRILL . . .

OF BEING IN SOLE COMMAND OF YOUR OWN BOAT.

"I'M **NOT** GOING TO BE RESCUED BY BOB AND
VERA HARRINGTON."

SAFETY FIRST

MAKE SURE THAT YOUR VESSEL IS SEAWORTHY
BEFORE SETTING SAIL

MAKE SURE THAT EACH MEMBER OF YOUR CREW IS
WEARING A LIFE JACKET

AVOID WEIRS

DO NOTHING THAT MAY ALARM OR ANNOY BATHERS

ALWAYS STEP RIGHT INTO THE CENTRE OF A SMALL BOAT

ALWAYS CARRY ENOUGH FUEL – IT IS DIFFICULT TO
OBTAIN AT SEA

AND NEVER MAKE ANY SIGNALS THAT MAY BE
MISTAKEN FOR A DISTRESS CALL

LISTEN CAREFULLY TO WEATHER FORECASTS

AND ABOVE ALL . . .

GIVE YOUR FRIENDS ON SHORE PRECISE DETAILS OF WHERE
YOU INTEND TO SAIL

*　　　*　　　*

"I DON'T KNOW WHAT IT MEANS BUT IT'S A
FOUR-LETTER WORD."

THE INTERNATIONAL CODE OF SIGNALS

I AM UNDERGOING A SPEED TRIAL

MAN OVERBOARD

I REQUIRE A TUG

STOP YOUR VESSEL

I HAVE SOMETHING IMPORTANT TO COMMUNICATE

I AM MANOEUVRING WITH DIFFICULTY

I AM IN NEED OF A PILOT

THIS VESSEL IS ABOUT TO DEPART

COMMUNICATE WITH ME

STOP CARRYING OUT YOUR INTENTIONS

I HAVE LOST MY BATHING COSTUME

*   *   *

"A CURSE ON THAT SELF-STEERING GEAR."

Rules of The Road For Sailors

CLEAN OFF ALL BARNACLES – THEY WILL SLOW DOWN
YOUR PROGRESS

KEEP WELL CLEAR OF ROCKS WHEN LEAVING HARBOUR

ORGANISE THE DOG WATCH

CHECK YOUR CRAFT FOR STOWAWAYS

BEWARE OF UNDERTOW

BE PREPARED FOR SUDDEN SQUALLS

AND IF YOU RUN INTO FOG – GIVE ONE LONG BLAST

IF YOU FIND YOURSELF IN SERIOUS TROUBLE –
HAVE SOMEONE READY TO BAIL YOU OUT

ABANDON SHIP ONLY AS A LAST RESORT

✳   ✳   ✳

"IF ANYONE HEARS THE ENGINE, WE'LL BE OSTRACIZED
AT THE CLUB."

GETTING THE WIND UP

THE BEAUFORT SCALE

FORCE O

DO NOT GET IMPATIENT – YOU COULD BE
BECALMED FOR WEEKS

FORCE 1-2

YOU WERE WARNED TO CARRY A
SPARE SET OF CHARTS

FORCE 3-4   YOU'RE GLAD SHE BROUGHT
HER MOTHER ALONG NOW

FORCE 5-6 — AND MOST OF THAT'S
RAW SEWAGE

FORCE 7-8   YOUR DINNER **WAS** IN THE OVEN

FORCE 9-10

IT'S GOING TO BE DICEY GETTING
HER HOME UP THE A.1.

FORCE 11-12   DO NOT WORRY – YOUR HOUSE
BLEW DOWN ANYWAY

✳   ✳   ✳

"THEY'LL ALLOW ME TO BURY YOU AT SEA BUT NOT IN
THESE WATERS, I'M AFRAID."

SEA FEVER

"DO YOU HAVE ANY CAVIAR?"

"I'M SORRY MATE BUT IT'S A
SINGLE-HANDED RACE."

"IF YOU DON'T STOP SLIMMING, I'LL HAVE TO LOOK
FOR FRESH CREW"

HELLO! THE CARGO'S SHIFTED

"I DON'T KNOW WHY YOU RACE WHEN YOU'RE
SUCH A DAMN POOR LOSER"

"**NOW** CAN WE START A FAMILY?"

"MY GOD, JACKSON! WE'RE NOT GOING TO MAKE IT"

"YOU SINGLE-HANDED CHAPS ARE ALL THE SAME."

"OH! FOR PITY'S SAKE LET HIM LIGHT IT."

"THAT WAS A NEAR THING, MAVIS"

"REMEMBER THAT CRUMP AT THE TRAFFIC LIGHTS?"

"WHAT A STUPID PLACE TO PUT AN OIL RIG!"

"NAVIGATION'S EASY – JUST FOLLOW THE
SEWAGE BACK HOME."

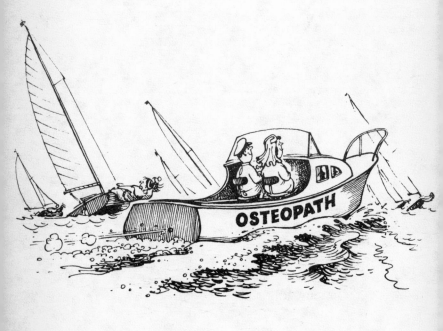

"YOU CAN ALWAYS TELL WHEN IT'S COWES WEEK"

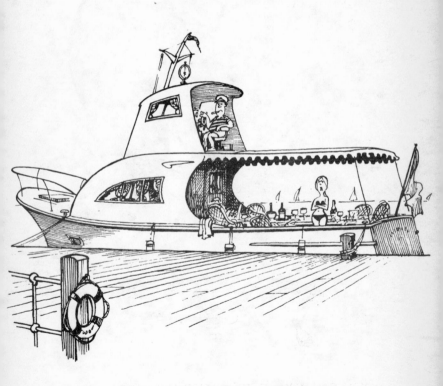

"THE DAILY WOMAN'S LATE AGAIN!"

"WHO'S WEARING STILETTO HEELS?"

"HE HATES DOING THE WEEDING."

"THEY'VE BEEN DONE! THEY'VE ALL BEEN DONE."

"KNEE DEEP IN SAWDUST AND SHAVINGS ALL WINTER –
AND FOR WHAT?"

Justice

Harry Brighouse

polity

First published in 2004 by Polity Press

Reprinted 2008 (twice)

Polity Press
65 Bridge Street
Cambridge CB2 1UR, UK

Polity Press
350 Main Street
Malden, MA 02148, USA

ISBN 978 0 7456 2596 6 (paperback)
ISBN 978 0 7456 2595 9 (hardback)

A catalogue record for this book is available from the British Library.

Typeset in 10.5 on 12 pt Sabon
by SNP Best-set Typesetter Ltd, Hong Kong
Printed and bound in Great Britain by MPG Books Ltd., Bodmin, Cornwall

For further information on Polity, visit our website: www.polity.co.uk

Contents

Preface

Justice is one of the central virtues of any social order. It matters enormously how we distribute the burdens required to maintain social organization and the benefits that accrue from it, because none of us should suffer worse lives from being treated wrongly by others, and none of us should benefit from wrong treatment of others. Although it sometimes seems as if contemporary political debates are dominated by self-interest, on the one hand, and technical details, on the other, it matters a great deal to a great many people that they live in just social arrangements. This book is about what it would be for social arrangements to be just.

I make no claims to completeness: the book focuses on the dominant theories of justice in contemporary political theory, but it does not survey the whole contemporary literature. Instead I have picked out the central theories and the central issues, and subjected them to fairly detailed discussions. There are three reasons for this. First, I think the reader learns more about the topic by seeing how positions are elaborated and disputed than by simply being given a brief overview of a great deal of literature. Second, I have designed the book to focus on a relatively small number of easily accessible books and articles so that it can be read alongside them. Even the best introductory volumes cannot substitute for direct acquaintance with the real thing. Third, although this volume is self-standing, I hope that readers who read it that way will see it as an invitation to, rather than alternative to, the literature beyond the literature it discusses. At the end of the book I provide a brief guide to an expanded literature which I hope the interested reader will pursue.

My choice of theories has been guided by three considerations. First, I want to provide an account of the main kinds of theories of justice prevailing in contemporary political philosophy. Second, I want to use versions of those theories that have had influence beyond the disciplinary confines of political philosophy. Increasingly students in the social sciences and even in the other humanities are expected to be acquainted with the work of Amartya Sen, Martha Nussbaum, Will Kymlicka and John Rawls.

I'd like to make a couple of comments on how to read the book. Each chapter has a discrete topic and could be read alone. But the book does build from the beginning, and I frequently make reference back to ideas from previous chapters. This reflects the state of the contemporary debate – on the whole, theorists in later chapters are responding to theorists in earlier chapters. The one chapter that could be skipped is chapter 1, but I do not recommend that the novice in political theory does so because it contains a long and helpful discussion of the methods of political philosophy that are used in subsequent chapters. Read the whole book.

But read it sceptically. This is an *opinionated* introduction to theories of justice. I believe that some of the theories I discuss have much more going for them than others do, and I do not disguise that (though neither do I dwell on it). You may disagree – in fact, you'll probably enjoy the book and learn from it more if you do. This is not a bland survey of views, designed to allow you to answer the Trivial Pursuit questions about contemporary philosophical theories of justice. It seeks to engage your powers of reason as you join in the collective project of working out what is the best theory of justice.

I wrote the book over about four years, of which I lived two in the United States and two in the United Kingdom. The moves to and from England slowed my progress, but provided me with two very different kinds of stimulus. I wrote a good deal of the manuscript while sitting on the Oxford City Bus Company's X90 service, and almost all of it while listening to BBC Radio 2. I'm grateful to the X90 drivers for their casual politeness and devious driving, and to whoever it was who decided to turn Radio 2 into the best music radio station imaginable. Adam Swift did not read the manuscript, but a great deal of my thinking about these matters has changed thanks to conversations with him – however, I should emphasize particularly strongly that he is not responsible for the results. I'm especially grateful to some of the students in the various sections of my upper-division Political Philosophy course at the University of Wisconsin, Madison, who have endured versions of these chapters, and to the students in my political philosophy reading groups and Values in Society MA module at the Institute of Education in London. Dianne Gereluk, Muna Golmohamad, Kats Katayama, Janet Orchard, Paul Severn, Lorella Terzi and Carrie Winstanley all helped me in numerous ways, as did my colleague Elaine Unterhalter; the book is much better for their interaction with the ideas as I developed them. Dale Murray made valuable comments especially on chapters 4 and 5. I'm also grateful to Michael Blake for immensely helpful comments, as well as to the other reviewer for Polity, whose kindness made his scepticism the more palatable. Louise Knight has been a model of patience with an author who must have been very frustrating to work with. Thanks, Louise. Most of all, as usual, I'm grateful to Lynn Glueck for everything, and to Maddy, and now Maisy, for slowing me down.

1
Introducing Justice

Justice

It will help to start out by making a few distinctions about justice, so as to specify precisely what the subject matter of this book is. The first known writing about justice comes down to us from the ancient Greek philosophers. It was common in their time to apply the adjective 'just' both to city states and to individual men. Indeed, it is only quite recently that the phrase 'a just man' has fallen out of use (replaced, I think, by the phrase 'an ethical man'). Plato, in *The Republic*, develops an account of justice in the state which he then uses as a model for describing justice in the individual. People organize into cities (states) because they cannot be self-sufficient, so they will more efficiently have their needs met in society with others. The city has three classes – the rulers, the soldiers and the citizens. The rulers and soldiers have specific functions and virtues, and justice is achieved when all parties develop their specific virtues and perform their functions well. The just city is, then, like a flourishing or thriving organism, in which each part plays its specified role well.

The just individual is modelled on the just city state. Like the city, the soul has three parts – the rational, the spirited and the appetitive. The just man is defined not in terms of how well he abides by the strictures of the city state, but by how well the three parts of his soul perform their particular functions. So the spirited part of the soul should be appropriately courageous, the rational part appropriately wise, and all three parts of the soul should be moderate.

To the modern mind it seems odd to evaluate an individual's status as a 'just' person in terms of how well their internal constitution mirrors that of the just state. In so far as we think of people as just or unjust, we tend to make that judgement about their relationship to the state – those who either infringe the law or act in such ways as to undermine the rule of law might be impugned as unjust. But Plato and other ancient thinkers thought of justice as a much more comprehensive aspect of people than we would – they mean something more like 'moral' or 'flourishing'. Anyway, the purpose of introducing Plato's approach is to distinguish matters of personal justice from matters of social, or political, justice. My focus in this book, following the modern tendency, is on the justice or otherwise of social institutions.

A second common distinction is between distributive and retributive justice. Distributive justice concerns the way in which what Rawls calls 'the benefits and burdens of social cooperation' are distributed among people, whereas retributive justice concerns the appropriate treatment of those who violate the laws and norms of society. In this case 'justice' is probably systematically ambiguous, and it is clear only from context whether someone is using it to talk about distribution or retributive issues. But they are quite different (though not unrelated) topics, and my focus here will be on distributive questions. The fundamental question is this: how, and to what end, should a just society distribute the various benefits (resources, opportunities and freedoms) it produces, and the burdens (costs, risks and unfreedoms) required to maintain it?

Conflicting values

Answering this question requires us to make judgements about the relative importance of the different benefits and burdens, and the relative importance of different values. In public debate about values a common strategy is to assume that when one has shown that two values conflict in some circumstances, and one is more important than the other, something has been settled. But that is, in fact, rarely the case. Consider the simple, and common, view that freedom and equality conflict, so we have to plump for one over the other. On any natural understanding of freedom and of equality, that seems to be true. If Rodney and Charles are equally well off, and we want to ensure that they remain equally well off, and either of them wants to be better off than the other, then we shall have to either restrict their freedom to engage in remunerated labour, or ensure that they cannot benefit financially from it (which requires taxing them, and redistributing the proceeds). This shows the instability of strict equality of wealth, and it also establishes that freedom and equality conflict. But demonstrating a conflict shows neither that freedom matters more, nor that equality does not matter at all. For example, we might think that it would be wrong, all things considered, to restrict freedom to achieve equality as needed, but still believe that a world in which Rodney and Charles refrained from wanting and trying to be better off than one another would be better than a world in which they competed for unequal positions. In other words, we might think that freedom trumps equality, but still think that equality matters morally, somewhat. Another response to the observed conflict would be to say that certain freedoms matter enormously, but that other freedoms do not fundamentally matter; and that the important freedoms must not be violated for the sake of equality, but that the unimportant freedoms may be. So, for example, we might think that as long as someone can benefit a reasonable amount from their own decision to work more hours, or take certain risks with their capital, their freedom as an economic agent is adequately protected, and it is morally acceptable to redistribute some of their gains for the benefit of others. Or we might think that no measures would be acceptable if they prevented parents from enjoying flourishing relationships with their children, but that the liberty to send one's child to the school of one's choice was not important enough to override our concern with equality.

A similar argument against equality is often made by appeal to the importance of efficiency and its conflict with equality. Economic equality is opposed because achieving it has bad effects on efficiency, in that individuals would have no incentive to be more innovative and productive, since they would not reap the benefits of their behaviour. So, the story goes, equality would make us all worse off than we would be under inequality.

In fact there is very little evidence that economies with relatively egalitarian net incomes (like Sweden, the Netherlands and Germany) do worse in the long run than economies with relatively inegalitarian net incomes (like the United States). But there must be something in the claim that equality would be bad for efficiency: it is easy to believe that under a strict regime of economic equality many people would work less hard, and take fewer productivity-enhancing economic risks. What follows from this, however? It does not follow directly that equality has no place in justice, for, again, two reasons. First, we would have to show that the economic benefits of inequality outweighed the non-economic benefits that equality might have. But even if we did this, we would not have shown that equality did not matter at all – if it really does have some non-economic benefits, those might be of a kind that justice takes into account.

So, observing that two values conflict, and even that one of those values is more important, is not sufficient to show that the less important value has no part to play in justice. A theory of justice has the task of assigning relative weights to different values to decide exactly which value should prevail and how in particular situations. Exactly how we go about this task I shall look at in the next chapter, and shall illustrate throughout the book.

The practical significance of justice

Is there any *practical* point in thinking about justice? A cynic might point out that in undemocratic countries rulers can do as they please, only within the constraints necessary to keep themselves in power. In democratic countries, by contrast, politicians try to please voters, who are using their votes to try to secure their own interests. What role could a theory of justice play in such a world? Not, surely, an action-guiding role, except for a few idealists whose ability to influence events will usually be limited.

There is, of course, some truth in the cynic's outlook. Most of us most of the time pay at least some attention to our own interests, and will attempt to protect them. But even conceding a great deal to the cynic, we can observe that in both undemocratic and democratic regimes there are frequent occasions when political actors might want recourse to a theory of justice. Most obviously, when an undemocratic regime is unstable, and citizens discover they have the power to change the regime, they may well be spurred to actions by motivations more noble than their own individual interests. They frequently deploy some ideals of justice not just to rally support for their actions, but also to guide them: to ensure that the ensuring regime will be better, that is, more just, than the one they are replacing. In such situations it is better for them to have well-justified views about justice than for them to have confused or wrongheaded views. Less obviously, there are many situations in the ordinary course of life within democracies where voters or interest groups have to choose among policies which are equally good for them, or which bear very little on their interests. In such situations justice is free to guide them.

But I'm not sure we should even concede so much to the cynic. People have very complex motivational structures, and while in favourable circumstances their motivations are often constrained by the inclination to ensure that their own interests will not be badly damaged, people are often moved in significant part by moral ideals. They are more energetic and effective, perhaps, if those moral ideals mesh well with their sense of what will be to their own benefit; but even when they do not mesh well, many people can do as they see that justice requires.

We can point to some historical events, especially in the modern period, in which self-interest does not seem to have been a force which drove out considerations of justice, and even in which awareness of philosophical thinking about justice was of value. Most strikingly, the founders of the

American nation deployed ideas drawn from John Locke's theory of justice in their design of the US Constitution; throughout Eastern Europe in the period following the fall of the Berlin Wall constitutional design was similarly influenced by thinking about justice, and not just by the self-interest of the framers, or their desire to favour particular political constituencies (though those motivations also had some effect).

Justice, social science and policy

Why would a book on justice qualify for a series on Key Concepts in the Social Sciences? Most of the disagreements in the social sciences are highly technical in nature; what social scientists are interested in is describing and explaining social processes, and for that they need fundamentally explanatory concepts, not normative concepts such as justice. But in fact what counts as an interesting problem for some purposes turns on what one thinks about justice, especially when one is doing social science that one hopes to be of use for policymakers.

Think of some of the debates about social mobility. Scholars of social mobility disagree about how best to conceive of classes or strata. They differ in particular in how much relative weight to assign to occupational type, education level and income. Now one obvious, and legitimate, consideration here will be which variables they can actually get data about. But assuming that they can get good data about a good number of variables, it makes sense then to consider the following question: why would social mobility matter from the perspective of justice? If in answering this question you found that it mattered a great deal that children's prospects were not influenced by their parents' income and wealth, but that it did not matter much if their prospects were influenced by their parents' level of education, it would make sense to give more weight to income than to education in conceiving of class.

Policymakers should have a particular interest in justice when deciding what kind of social scientific studies to commission for policy purposes. Suppose that you are running an

Education Ministry, and are trying to figure out how best to spend a sudden increase in resources. Obviously, you should try to spend it on effective programmes. But different programmes are liable to have different effects on different kinds of students; it will be a rare policy (or package of policies) that benefits all students equally. If justice demands that we maximize the achievement of the lowest-achieving students, that might require different policies than if justice demands that we maximize average student achievement. Suppose justice requires giving priority to the achievement of low achievers. Then you will want to commission studies of policies and programmes that you have reason to believe might benefit the low achievers rather than those which might benefit total achievement.

Of course, politicians will typically be unwilling to concede in public that there are trade-offs between benefit to the low achievers and overall benefit – they like to claim that their policies are for the benefit of everyone. Sometimes they prefer to use apparently non-normative concepts to justify policies. So, for example, recent documents from the World Bank have deployed the concepts of human and social capital in justifying various interventions in the developing world (see, e.g., World Bank 2001). Human capital consists of the skills and knowledge embodied in people, and the idea is that economies will be more productive (other things being equal) if people are better educated. Social capital consists of the relationships of trust and reciprocity that enable people to interact productively without the high transaction and monitoring costs involved in making and enforcing precise contracts; and again, the idea is that economies are more productive and the quality of life is better if there are higher levels of social capital. Human capital and social capital are empirically observable, and they both obviously matter a great deal, so it is tempting to use their development as the sole justification of a policy. But consider the task of increasing the stock of human capital. Different policies will have effects on different people. For example, maximizing the total stock of human capital in the short to medium term might involve focusing on developing a domestic intellectual and technocratic elite, and providing sufficient material incentives to keep them from emigrating (and taking their capital with them). This might do very little for the least advantaged within the society; it might, nevertheless, be justified, but whether it is or not will turn on what justice requires concerning the distribution of resources, education, and so on. The trade-offs between benefits to some and benefits to others are unavoidable. Many politicians privately understand very well that the real world contains trade-offs, and their civil servants are bound to focus attention as those trade-offs demand. But without a normative theory of justice to tell them which variables matter, they cannot know what information they need to find.

The plan of the book

The book proceeds as follows. In chapter 2 I discuss some methodological issues in theorizing about justice. If, as I claim, the task is to demonstrate the relationships between a cluster of values, how on earth can we do that? Not, certainly, by collecting empirical data and formulating hypotheses explaining the relationships between the data. In this chapter I explain some of the methods political philosophers use to think abut justice, and defend their use. I also defend a constraint on theorizing – that it must make realistic assumptions about what is feasible given the limits of human nature.

In chapter 3 I present and discuss John Rawls's theory of justice as fairness. This is the longest, and most difficult, chapter, but both the length and the complexity are unavoidable. Rawls's theory was developed in the 1960s and first defended at length in his 1971 book *A Theory of Justice*. All theorizing about justice in the English language since that time operates within a framework set by Rawls. Even if a theorist disagrees, absolutely, with everything Rawls says, the theorist has to explain why, so it is worth having as full a grasp of the theory as an introductory text like this can provide.

In chapter 4 I look at what has been called the 'capability' approach developed by Amartya Sen and Martha Nussbaum. The capability approach was originally developed as an alternative to gross domestic product and other income-based measures of how well off different countries are relative to each other. Sen's insight is that money is not always a good indicator of how well off people truly are, and that their real freedom to do things that they have reason to value might be a better measure. But, in saying that, he is advancing a normative position – an idea about what matters from the point of view of justice – and this chapter explores the arguments for that position.

The theories surveyed in chapters 3 and 4 demand considerable redistribution away from the kinds of economic outcomes we would expect from the operation of relatively free capital and labour markets. In particular, both theories demand that the return to people's talents be limited in various ways. Chapter 5 looks at two theories which object to the large-scale redistribution licensed by the previous theories. Milton Friedman argues that a proper understanding of the role of freedom in a democratic society severely limits the scope of redistribution, and Robert Nozick argues that respect for persons requires that we permit individuals to benefit from their productive activity: he says that 'taxation is on a par with forced labour'.

Whereas the classical liberal and libertarian theories surveyed in chapter 5 complain that the egalitarian theories of Rawls and Sen are insufficiently individualistic, the group-rights theorists I look at in chapter 6 claim that such theories are too individualistic. I survey arguments that justice requires that groups, as well as individuals, should be the bearers of some basic rights, and that in some circumstances some groups may be entitled to rights that other groups are not entitled to. I look in detail at the work of Will Kymlicka, whose work on group-differentiated rights has been extremely influential on policymakers and non-governmental organizations the world over.

Chapter 7 has an institutional focus. Having presented some of the main contending theories, I look at how they apply to three policy issues, each of which arises in some form or another in many developed countries. The first is affirmative action – should members of historically disadvantaged groups be given preference in access to jobs or places in higher education? The second concerns what measures, if any, the state is required to take to promote social mobility. And the third concerns the division of labour in the household and the inequality of position between men and women in the paid workforce. Each of the contending theories is tested by what it says, or should say, about these issues.

Chapter 7 paves the way for the following chapter. Most of the theories I survey recognize that in principle some areas of human activity should not be judged by the standards of justice, and should be regarded essentially as private. Many of the disagreements over issues arising in chapter 7 reveal differences between the theories about what kinds of behaviour and problem should count as being in the private sphere. So in chapter 8 I look at some attempts to make the private/public distinction much more problematic than the major contenders take it to be. I look, in particular, at G.A. Cohen's objection to Rawls's claim that the Basic Structure of society (rather than the choices and actions of individuals) is the primary subject of justice, and at Nancy Fraser's theory which tries to integrate the values of distribution and of recognition.

Finally, in the conclusion, I shall note some of the common ground of the several theories surveyed, and also explore some conservative reflections on justice.

2
Ideal Theory and Institutional Feasibility

Many students, on their first encounter with political philosophy, find it frustrating. It can seem excessively abstract and technical. It sometimes appears to be difficult for the sake of seeming difficult. If you come to political philosophy with a concern about contemporary political issues, it can seem disappointing. You are interested in globalization, gender inequality, third-world debt, capitalism; but philosophers seem interested only in the nature of rights, or what goods should be distributed equally, or the relationship between rights and responsibilities. They also often seem completely unconcerned with what their theories imply for the world that they, and we, live in.

If you feel that way, I have some sympathy, and one theme of this book is that political philosophers should be more concerned than they sometimes seem to be with political institutions. But I only have *some* sympathy. In fact, many of the very same philosophers whose highly abstract work you will encounter in a first political theory class also write extensively on what their theories mean for the real world; the impression given is partly an issue of what is selected for introductory classes. And despite the misleading impression that selection gives of the field, it is the right selection, because there is not much point in thinking about how theories apply in the world until you have learned a good deal about how theories are designed and how to engage with them philosophically on their own terms. The best way of learning how to do political philosophy is to 'watch' it being done, and in this book I am going to present a selection of important theories of justice while commenting on the way those theories are developed and argued about. First I want to introduce some of the philosophical methods that are commonly used, defend their use, and then look at how considerations about the real world should constrain our theorizing.

What is philosophy? It is the systematic study of questions the answers to which cannot be determined simply by gathering observational data about the world and making hypotheses about those data. 'Is the earth flat?' is not a philosophical question, because ultimately it has to be addressed through observation. 'What is the nature of knowledge?', by contrast, is philosophical. Without experiences we could not address it, to be sure (we'd not be alive), but its answer does not rest on observation. Philosophical questions may well have determinate answers; there is a truth about them – but theoretical, rather than empirical, reason is the means to arriving at the truth. Moral philosophy is the field within philosophy that asks questions about how we should live our lives, and what constitutes goodness. It encompasses large general questions such as 'What makes a flourishing human life?', 'Does the value of actions lie in their consequences or the motives behind them?' and 'Are states of affairs or the characters of persons the ultimate bearers of value?', and also much more local questions such as 'Is abortion morally wrong?' and 'Is it ever right to lie?'

Theorizing about justice falls under the subfield of moral philosophy which is concerned primarily with how we relate to other people through social institutions: political philosophy. Theories of justice tell us what principles should guide us when designing social institutions, reforming them and living within them. How do we establish conclusions about these matters? The method that most of the philosophers discussed in the following pages follow is what John Rawls has called the method of *reflective equilibrium*. This method invites us to develop a theory of justice in the following way. We list our considered judgements about particular cases, and look at whether they fit together consistently. Where we find inconsistencies, we reject those judgements in which we have least reason to be confident (for example, those in which we have reason to suspect there is an element of self-interest pressing us to the conclusion we have reached). We also list the principles we judge suitable to cover cases, and look through those principles for inconsistency, again rejecting those concerning which we have least reason to be confident in our judgements. Then we look at the particular judgements and the principles in the light of one another. Are there inconsistencies? Do some of the principles look less plausible in the light of the weight of considered judgements, or vice versa?

Of course, all that this method gives us is, at best, a consistent set of judgements. But if we engage in the process collectively, in conversation with others who are bound by similar canons of rationality, we can have increasing confidence in the truth of the outcomes. Other people can bring out considerations we had not noticed; they can alert us to weaknesses in our own judgements; they can force us to think harder and better. If we converge on conclusions about particular cases with people with whom we otherwise disagree a great deal, we should have more confidence in our judgement. We cannot ever be certain that we have arrived at the final true theory of justice. But this method at least gives us a way of making some progress.

What do I mean by 'judgements about particular cases' and 'principles'? An autobiographical comment will help, one which, I'm afraid, does not reflect particularly well on me. In the late 1970s I held a pre-theoretical view that, I think, was quite common among British teenagers with my political outlook, which was that there was no reason to grant free speech to racists, or anyone with anti-social views, and that it was entirely fine for the government to censor offensive films. So, the principle I held was something like this: 'Governments should have the power to censor expression when it meets some objective criteria for being anti-social.' One morning I turned on the radio and heard Jimmy Young (a DJ) announce that he was soon going to be talking to a Church of England vicar who was trying to have a new film, *Rimbaud*, banned from his local cinema. My reaction was outrage – 'How dare this busy-bodying minister try to shut down a film about the great homosexual French poet Rimbaud?' (The judgement was about an individual case: 'It is wrong to censor *this* film.') When the discussion began, however, it turned out that the vicar objected not to its portrayal of homosexuality, but to its excessive violence – it was, of course, called *Rambo*, not *Rimbaud*, and starred Sylvester Stallone (who would have been an eccentric choice for Rimbaud). The film was entirely devoid of reference to homosexuality or poetry, and had I heard the vicar without having been confused about his topic, I would have agreed with every word he said. (The judgement about the individual case I *would* have had: 'It is fine to censor *this* film.') There was not, in fact, a conflict between my principle and my judgement about the individual cases, but being forced by the situation to think through the principle and both judgements together, I realized that I had no good grounds for my adherence to the principle, and have ever since had a much more liberal (and, dare I say, rational) attitude toward freedom of expression.

How do we isolate our judgements about particular cases? Usually we are not so lucky as to be forced to think things through by a disc jockey. Two methods are common in theorizing about justice, and I shall describe them both. The first is the thought experiment. Thought experiments tend to be very unrealistic inventions, in which the theorist imagines a situation in which implementing a principle has an unacceptable consequence, or in which two judgements conflict that we previously thought were consistent. Often the thought experiment is supposed to be analogous to a real-life case in all relevant respects, but shows up the inapplicability of some judgement to the real-life case. The most famous, and in my view the greatest, thought experiment in moral philosophy is Judith Jarvis Thomson's 'violinist' case, in her paper 'A Defense of Abortion' (Thomson 1971). Thomson draws an analogy between the case of abortion where the prospective mother has conceived as a result of rape, and the following case: a famous violinist is dying of a rare blood disease, which can only by cured by having you (the reader) hooked up to him for a certain amount of time (say nine months) so that he can use your body to cleanse his kidney. No-one else will do – because, say, you and he are the only people in the world with a certain blood group. A Society of Music Lovers takes it upon itself to kidnap you and hook you up to the violinist. When you awake you find yourself able to unhook yourself and walk away. Thomson asks whether the violinist has the right that you remain hooked up to him, and assumes that most of her readers will say 'no'. But, she says, what is the difference between this case and the case of abortion where the pregnancy arose from rape? The prospective mother is being used by the foetus, and only she will do for its purposes. She is not in that situation out of choice: she was forced into it by someone else (not, admittedly, the foetus, but nor did the violinist force you into being hooked up to him). So, abortion, at least in the case of rape, is not wrong.

Thomson deploys other thought experiments to show that abortion is permissible in a much wider range of cases, but I want to focus on what this, very limited, thought experiment actually shows. When I teach Thomson's paper I find that most of the students who oppose abortion do not get persuaded that there is anything acceptable about abortion. But in fact Thomson's paper is less directed at showing there is a right to abortion than to showing something quite different: that whatever is wrong with abortion has nothing to do with the right to life of the foetus. Whereas supporters and opponents of abortion rights frequently argue over whether the foetus has a right to life, Thomson concedes at the start that it does. Her thought experiment is so striking because the violinist, who is supposed to be analogous to the foetus, is an adult, with all the rights and moral standing that adults typically have. When we say that we are entitled to walk away from the violinist, we do so in the knowledge that he is an adult who certainly has a right to life, and that he will die if we walk away, and, crucially, that even though he will die, we will not be violating his right to life. Opponents of abortion believe the foetus has a right to life, and that the violinist has a right to life. They are not forced by Thomson's thought experiment to give up the view that abortion is wrong, even in the case where pregnancy arises from rape; but if they want to say that it is permissible to walk away from the violinist, they are forced to look for some other grounds than the right to life of the foetus for justifying the wrongness of abortion. In my own experience I find that students are quite ingenious about finding other grounds for supporting what they believe, but what they have given up is the central slogan of the anti-abortion movement: 'right to life'. Sure, foetuses have rights to life, but that cannot be why abortion is wrong.

I've dwelled on this example because it neatly displays both the power and the limits of thought experiments. Good thought experiments are powerful because they can force us to interrogate judgements we had previously simply assumed, and show them to be groundless. They can be especially powerful in highlighting conflicts between disparate principles. Thomson has in mind a particular combination of views which is commonly found, but which she thinks cannot be sustained:

(a)   the idea that women have no right to abortion;
(b)   the idea that people do not have extensive duties to help strangers; and
(c)   the idea that people have strong rights to control over their own bodies.

She adheres to the third of these ideas, and sounds, in the article, as if she adheres to the second; but she shows that if you do adhere to these two, you cannot consistently hold on to the first.

Thought experiments are limited because they tend, alone, not to support substantive conclusions about what is right and wrong, but only show that certain kinds of reasons do, or do not, support such substantive conclusions. The other common method for isolating particular judgements is discussion of particular real-world cases and case studies. US-based political theorists have a long tradition of exploring the reasoning offered in Supreme Court cases, for example: in fact much of the theorizing about the content of the right to freedom of expression (about which a little more below) in the United States engages directly with the reasoning offered in landmark cases where the Court first imposed, and later gradually lifted, various restrictions on expression. A series of cases form the basis for theorizing about the extent and meaning of the right to freedom of conscience (see Galston 2002; Weithman 2000). In countries which lack that rich source of opinions, practical political dilemmas often form the case studies on which political theorists can reflect. One recent book, in exploring the difficult question of the extent to which it is permissible for parents to act to confer advantages on their own children, interrogates the reasons offered by Harriet Harman, then a senior politician in the British Labour Party, in defence of her decision to send her child to an academically selective school (Swift 2003); other theorists start from thinking about the public reasons offered for decisions concerning the allocation of healthcare resources at the micro or macro level (Buchanan et al. 2000; Daniels 1985), the justification of particular wars (Moellendorf 2000; Walzer 1977), and disputes about what governments in multilingual nations should do for linguistic minorities (Kymlicka 1995).

Although most theorists tend to work with one rather than the other of these methods, both are extremely valuable, and they complement each other well. There is a sense, which I shall describe in the next section, in which political principles must be feasible in order to count as good principles. Real-world cases help to ground the theorist in reality, and to give us a sense (but only a sense) of what is feasible. At the same time, theorists who work exclusively with case studies could easily be fooled into having a very restricted sense of what is feasible: some American democratic theorists, for example, talk as if the peculiar circumstances of contemporary American life should constrain our ultimate ideals. They are wrong: they may well constrain what would be a good strategy to achieve a better America, but they do not constrain our ultimate principles (Galston 2002). The method of thought experiments has almost exactly the reverse advantages and drawbacks. The thought experiment as a method was developed in non-normative areas of philosophy which do not have to worry about what is feasible, and the method can therefore be deceptive: we are allowed to imagine things that are physically, and therefore historically, impossible; obviously when we do so we are not observing any kind of feasibility constraint. On the other hand, the thought experiment, used carefully, can alert us to possibilities that are otherwise masked.

Both methods can seem highly abstract and technical, and can put off readers in the manner I described at the beginning of the chapter. So I want to defend the importance of abstract philosophizing, before going on to explain the importance of attention to the world.

Think, again, about the right to freedom of expression. Most of us think of it as a basic right that a just society has an obligation to protect. But what does it mean, or, more precisely, what expression does it protect? It cannot, surely, mean that *all* expression must be protected. Consider the practice of knee-capping, which was regularly used by the Irish Republican Army in the 1980s against police informers and unauthorized drug dealers. Knee-capping consists of shooting the victim in the knees so that the cartilage shatters irreparably. A central purpose of knee-capping is to 'send a message' to other potential informers and dealers that they should refrain. It is, in fact, an act of expression, but no-one believes that it should be protected. An immediate reaction might be to say that all acts of expression should be protected except those which are illegal. But, of course, that allows the government to pick and choose what expression will be protected: if it makes a law against public prayer, then public prayer is illegal, and so does not merit protection on this account.

The only way to figure out which acts of expression should be protected and which should not is by philosophizing, abstractly, about what fundamental interests are served by protecting expression and how important those interests are relative to others which may be jeopardized by particular kinds of expression. This is a technical and abstract process, and may involve us in thinking about hypothetical, as well as real, cases (some excellent examples can be found in Cohen 1993; Langton 1993; and Scanlon 1972).

Think also about the age of consent for sex. Our standard thinking about rights (which I shall assume throughout most of this book) is that rights-bearers are assumed to be self-governing, autonomous persons, who are better at judging what is good for themselves than anyone else is. But young children are not like this. Older children, and adolescents, may be better than anyone else at judging what is best in some areas of their lives, and not as good in others. And we certainly do not all suddenly become better at judging what is good for us than are others overnight all at the same age. The age of consent for sex should be set in a way that treats everyone by the same standard, but should also accurately reflect the real interests we have in becoming self-determining adults. If the age is set too young, it risks exposing children to exploitation which will result in both immediate and long-term harm; if it is set too high, it risks imposing an oppressive standard. But establishing what constitutes harm and good judgement, and what it is reasonable to hold people responsible for, cannot be done by simply doing surveys or looking at the biological facts – it requires us to reflect philosophically, conjecturing principles and considering counter-examples to them.

However, political philosophizing sometimes seems to proceed without any attention to the facts about the world at all. Not all of it: there are, in fact, some terrific examples of philosophical attention to real-world problems, such as the justice of international relations and military intervention; rights to health and healthcare; affirmative action; the morality of abortion (see the Guide to Further Reading). But it is sometimes said that there is a clear distinction between ideal theory – working out what the principles of justice are, which can proceed without any reference to the facts – and the application of that theory to institutions. Our theory of justice, on this view, constitutes a regulative ideal, to which we should aspire even if we know that we cannot fully reach it. When designing institutions, we choose those that can best realize the principles we have offered, even if they cannot realize them fully.

I'm now going to draw on two different areas, and show why some of the facts about the world matter even for the process of devising abstract principles of justice. The particular facts that matter concern what is institutionally feasible. A principle of justice that could only be implemented through institutions which are not, in a sense I shall explain, feasible should, for that reason, be rejected. The reason is rather simple. There's a slogan in moral theory which says that 'ought implies can'. What this means is that individual agents are not obliged to do anything that it is literally impossible for them to do. So, for example, it would be nonsense to say that someone had an obligation to jump over the moon (even if, say, they had promised to do so), not only because it is hard to see that jumping could be a moral action, but also because it is literally impossible for them to perform the action. In William Styron's famous novel *Sophie's Choice*, Sophie is told that one of her children will be killed, and the other saved, and that she has to choose which will live. It is literally impossible for her to save both of her children, and there is therefore no obligation on her to save both her children (though there certainly would be such an obligation if it were possible for her to do that).

Principles of justice describe obligations which the members of society collectively have toward one another. 'Ought implies can' is a slightly more complex slogan in this case, and it is much harder for us to know what is possible in terms of the design of social institutions than in the case of individual action (though it is by no means simple even in the individual case). But the slogan still holds. Principles of justice which it is literally impossible to implement are, by virtue of that fact, false: they do not truly describe obligations.

I want to illustrate what this means by discussing two examples. The first draws on Allen Buchanan's work on the justice of secession (Buchanan 1998); the second draws on Andrew Levine's work on the justice of rewards in the labour market (Levine 1999).

Buchanan is concerned with the conditions under which it is just for a new state to secede from a previously existing state, as has recently happened with Czechoslovakia, Ethiopia and the states which used to constitute Yugoslavia. Buchanan distinguishes two main kinds of theory: Primary Right theories and Remedial Right Only theories. Primary Right theories say that there is a presumption in favour of secession, and that groups can secede from existing states as long as certain procedural conditions are met: for example, a majority for secession has been won in a plebiscite in the seceding territory. Remedial Right Only theories, by contrast, presume against secession: they say that it is only just for a territory to secede when inhabitants of the territory have suffered, and must expect, absent secession, to continue to suffer, some serious injustice (with injustice understood in terms which make no reference to the fact that the seceding territory has not been allowed to secede).

Buchanan sets up three criteria for evaluating these different kinds of theory:

1 *Minimal realism*: The theory under consideration must have 'some significant prospect of eventually being implemented through the actual processes by which international law is made and applied' (Buchanan 1998: 42).
2 *Consistency with morally progressive principles of international law*: The theory has to be consistent with those principles of international law that accord with justice.
3 *Absence of perverse incentives*: It must not be the case that recognizing the theory in international law would provide agents who wanted to avoid secession with incentives to commit injustices against, or otherwise harm, the inhabitants of territories claiming, or likely in the future to claim, the right to secede.

Buchanan has two main objections to Primary Right theories for our purposes. First, they are not minimally realistic – they license the break-up of states 'even when those states are perfectly performing what are generally recognized as the legitimating functions of states' (Buchanan 1998: 45). Think of the following theory of the right to secede, which we'll call 'the Associative Group' theory. It says that whenever a group which shares a lasting history of national identity has the practical capacity to run an independent state of its own, and the majority of that group has a lasting ambition for its own state, the group has the fundamental right to form its own state – the right to secede. This allows groups who are not being treated unjustly to secede even when they have no complaint of injustice against the state from which they secede. It is easy to see why existing states, which determine the content of international law, would be reluctant to allow law to be guided by such a theory. Furthermore, just states, at least, have a 'morally legitimate interest' in maintaining their integrity. Establishing and maintaining a more or less just state is a considerable institutional achievement, and there are no guarantees that either, let alone both, of the states consequent on a political divorce would be able to maintain an internally just polity.

But, more tellingly, Buchanan says that Primary Right theories establish perverse incentives. So suppose the Associative Group theory were written into international law. Any state which contained within it a group that had the ambition to secede would have an incentive to prevent that group from becoming capable of having a functioning state. It would have an incentive, for example, to perform various kinds of ethnic cleansing, or to ensure that the group could not amass significant resources; or to redesign its electoral system to discourage the political expression of the ambitions of the national group; or to prevent even limited self-government, for fear that this would give rise to expression of the ambition for, and development of the capacity for, more extensive self-government. This is (a) an incentive to behave unjustly but also (b) an incentive to behave (within the limits of justice) to frustrate the associative ends of individuals who comprise groups likely to come to have such a capability (Buchanan 1998: 52) (which is the ultimate value endorsed by an Associative Group theory). Even if the host state did nothing that was prohibited by justice more neutrally understood, it might still act in ways that frustrate the associative interests of the group in question: treating it badly, though not unjustly.

What Buchanan is doing is taking a principle which we find very appealing in certain contexts – that people should be able freely to associate on their own terms – and showing that if it were adopted as a principle applied to the formation and re-formation of nations it would make it more difficult for people to realize the good – free association – to which it appeals. He tacitly invokes the idea that if something is a good principle it should be one that can be publicly recognized and implemented in a way that produces the goods it promises. The Associative Group theory, he thinks, fails that test. So it should give way to some other principle or kind of principle. This is the method of reflective equilibrium in action: we see two appealing desiderata, discover a (surprising) conflict between them, and give one of them up.

Now, one natural way of avoiding Buchanan's objections is to say that the various versions of Primary Right theory are offered as part of ideal theory: we assume that justice holds in other arenas, and then say this is the principle which would be best adopted in such circumstances, not in the messy and unjust world we now inhabit. But there are two problems with this strategy. First, it does not address the problem described above that even a just state would have incentives to do bad things. But the second problem is that a theory of secession is only interesting in circumstances in which everything cannot be presumed to be just. Claims for secession are urgent in contexts in which injustice is present. If the theory of secession on offer is applicable only against a background in which it is assumed that all other institutions are justly arranged, it tells us nothing about how to evaluate all of the claims for secession we are likely to encounter.

Another way of avoiding Buchanan's objections to Primary Right theories is to say that the demand for minimal realism is too strong. The system of states is, after all, entirely arbitrary and so it could be said to have no standing legitimacy. Any group has as much claim to a state as the groups which currently have them – that is, none at all. Minimal realism makes it impossible for us to criticize the system of states as it is, at least in its broad outlines. Imagine what minimal realism of this kind would have required of a theory of justice in 1100 anywhere in the world.

I think this is a powerful objection to Buchanan's minimal realism requirement, at least as he states it. His minimal realism requirement skews the case against more demanding theories of secession, precisely because it gives existing states incentives for conservatism in their approach to the processes of international law. But this objection does not in any way vindicate Primary Right over Remedial Right Only theories, because the perverse incentives problem remains.

If Buchanan's minimal realism requirement is too strong, does this mean that philosophers need pay no attention at all to what is actually feasible in the world? I am now going to try to explain why I think an even more minimal realism is a reasonable requirement for political philosophers to observe. In service of developing this alternative I shall turn to Andrew Levine's argument for the inappropriateness of rewarding effort.

As we shall see in the course of chapters 3, 4 and 5, the dominant theories of justice in contemporary political philosophy challenge the common-sense association of merit with achievement. They point out that what you deserve ought to be connected with what you are responsible for, but then go on to show that many of the factors which influence achievement are factors for which we are not responsible. For example, we cannot think of ourselves as responsible for our natural talents – we are lucky, not responsible, for having them, and lucky too that they are valued as much as they are by other people. Similarly, the extent to which we have been educated is not something for which we are responsible – it reflects the means and choices of our parents and of the wider society that voted for the policymakers responsible for the education system. But our natural talents and our education are factors in our achievement. So we are not fully responsible for our achievements. However, some of these theories single out a factor which also influences achievement, and for which they do take us to be responsible: the degree of effort we put into our work. Social institutions, they say, should aim to reward effort, at least.

Levine argues against these theories, not by saying that they divorce contribution overly from reward (for example, because talent should be rewarded), but because they are insufficiently radical. Even effort, he says, has no claim to be rewarded.

One way of arguing for this is to say that we are not responsible for even our degree of effort. This is a remarkably powerful argument, but it is not Levine's. Levine argues instead that there is no way of identifying the contribution of effort to production, and there could not be such a way. Crucial to his argument is the observation that mere effort in any task is not worthy of reward. If Kenneth put lots of work into becoming a successful brain surgeon, and Clement puts exactly the same amount of work into becoming a mediocre tiddlywinks player, no-one is going to argue that Clement and Kenneth should be rewarded equally. Clement put his effort into developing a skill which (as it happens, for good reasons) is much less socially valued than the skill that Kenneth tried to develop; and if it is reasonable to hold people responsible for their degree of effort, it is also reasonable to hold them responsible for how they direct their efforts. It is effort directed at socially valued tasks that should be rewarded. But Levine looks at the way that actual firms in capitalist markets work, and notes (Levine 1999: 412) that effort is very rarely rewarded because, among other things, it would be too costly (if it were even possible) to gather information about it. What companies in fact do is try to find ways roughly to approximate actual and potential achievement. Furthermore, wage rates in the private sector are constrained by market prices (Levine 1999: 413). Two people working in different firms may exert the same degree of effort, but it would not be possible to reward them equally, even if we could measure their effort, because one firm commands higher prices than the other. On top of this, in the public sector it is impossible to gauge the value of effort to the enterprise of the organization. Anyway, if our ambition were to reward effort, rewarding it within but not across firms and sectors would be far from just. Finally, in order to exert socially useful effort, you have to have a job. But this is a scarce resource in capitalist economies (Levine 1999: 415–16). Consider two people, Julian and Sandy, who both apply for a highly paid and socially valued job with a law firm. They are both highly competitive candidates, but, basically on the toss of a coin, Julian gets the position. Julian is now in a position to reap the rewards for socially valued effort; Sandy is not, even though he would have put forth an equally high degree of socially valued effort if he had been given the job. Luck puts Julian in the position of being able to put forward socially valued effort. He is not responsible for that. It is impossible to reward socially valued effort, because it is impossible to identify it to the extent that people are responsible for it, so we should not do it. That is Levine's argument.

What I am particularly interested in is the structure of Levine's argument, rather than its substance. Maybe he is wrong that effort cannot be identified. But if he is right, then I think the argument works. It has the following basic structure:

- If we ought to do X, then it must be possible for us to do X.
- So if we ought to reward (socially valued) effort, it must be possible for us to reward (socially valued) effort.
- But it is not possible for us to reward (socially valued) effort.

- So it is not the case that we ought to reward (socially valued) effort.

There are two obvious ways to respond to Levine's argument. One is to deny the impossibility of identifying socially valued effort. If it is possible to identify effort, then, obviously, the argument does not succeed. The other response, more interesting for my present purpose, is to deny that 'ought implies can'. This response says that it doesn't have to be the case that we can fully implement a principle for that principle to be binding. Applying this response to Levine's case, we might say that we have very good reasons for thinking that effort is unlike other contributions to achievement, and that it merits reward. We cannot, admittedly, disentangle effort from the other contributory factors, but since we know that it, uniquely, merits reward, we know that we should design institutions to resemble *as closely as possible* those that would implement the ideal. This is not meaningless in practice. If it were true that effort, uniquely, commanded reward, we would have reasons to implement a high basic minimum wage; reform the education system so that neither individual ability nor parental wealth influenced how many resources went to any child's education; subsidize healthcare so that everyone was in a reasonable state to put forth effort, and so on.

There's something to this objection, but I don't think it succeeds. Suppose you held the view that effort was the only just grounds of reward, and that all other grounds of reward were unjust. And suppose you accepted that no system could reward it with complete success. Then you would have the view that some resources are inevitably going to be distributed unjustly. But, presumably, you would think there were more and less just ways of distributing that surplus. So, for example, if reward were in proportion to effort as far as possible and the remainder all went to white people, that might be more unjust than if reward were in proportion to effort to the same extent but the remainder was randomly distributed. But such a view amounts to a theory about what the maximally possible just distribution would be. An ideal theory that made no comment on this would be inadequate; but a theory which specified the maximally possible just distribution would be all that we could want.

In other words, at the very least it is reasonable to demand that a theory of justice attend to questions of what is institutionally feasible – something like Buchanan's minimal realism constraint. But, as we saw when discussing Buchanan's views, his actual minimal realism constraint seems excessively conservative; it demands that the theory be attentive to what is actually feasible right now, rather than to more general considerations of what would be institutionally feasible in alternative circumstances. To understand the general feasibility constraint on theories of justice, let's distinguish several possible meanings of the term 'feasible'.

Sometimes, when it is claimed that some principle is not institutionally feasible, what is meant is that there is no way that principle can be implemented right now: the balance of political forces is such that it is a fantasy to imagine politicians implementing it. This is the case for the principle of universal healthcare in the United States; and similarly for the principle that inequalities of private wealth should not influence inequalities of public power. Certainly, unfeasibility of a principle in that sense does not count against it, and accepting a feasibility constraint in this sense would be extremely conservative, disallowing many of the principled critiques of public institutions it is reasonable to make.

But sometimes when we say some principle is not institutionally feasible we mean something like this: 'Even in the best possible circumstances, in which people were willing to implement the principle, it would be impossible to implement it because it would be impossible to design institutions that incorporated the principle.' That, I take it, is the sense of unfeasibility Levine is relying on in his argument against rewarding effort. And if a principle is unfeasible in this sense, it seems right to think that it is, simply, a false principle. Think of how an argument about the principle would go. The advocate of the principle says, 'This is a true principle of justice, so we live in an unjust society, because our society falls short of the principle.' Her opponent retorts, 'But the principle cannot be implemented even in the best possible circumstances, so it is impossible for our society, or any other, to implement the principle.' 'Yes,' says the advocate, 'but that just means that the world is unavoidably an unjust place.' 'Well,' says the opponent, 'in that case justice has no bearing on what we should do. Injustice in that sense is nobody's fault, and not even the fault of "the system". What I have reason to care about is how far the world falls short of an ideal that it could actually meet, and how far it falls short of that ideal.' The opponent seems reasonable: in so far as justice commands us to do things we cannot do, it has no bearing on what we ought to do.

The feasibility constraint, then, as I propose it, is that 'No principle of justice can be a true principle if, in the most favourable circumstances possible, it would be impossible to implement that principle to the full extent demanded by its place in the theory of justice.' Before moving on I want to make one comment about how this should influence our thinking. It is hard to be confident even in claims concerning short-term political feasibility. I blithely said that universal healthcare in the United States is politically unfeasible in the short term; but in 1988 the vast majority of commentators believed the same thing about much more revolutionary changes in Eastern Europe. Certainly nobody in the West at that time believed that a unified democratic Germany was feasible within a few years without massive bloodshed. They were all wrong. However difficult it is to be confident in short-term political infeasibility claims, it is harder still to be confident in claims about the unfeasibility of a principle in highly favourable circumstances. While it is vital to think through, as far as possible, the institutional meaning of purported principles of justice, we should always be tentative in dismissing them on grounds of unfeasibility.

Each of the following four chapters is devoted to a theory, or a cluster of theories, of justice. I shall explain both the architecture of each theory, and the central arguments given in its defence, as well as some of the arguments presented against it. As I have said, it is not an unopinionated presentation: I think some of the arguments are good, others bad, and shall explain why; and these opinions about the arguments lead me to endorse some aspects of some of the theories and reject others. This is not inappropriate in an introductory text. I am introducing not only the theories of justice themselves, but also the techniques of argumentation about justice, and I suspect it would seem weird if I explained in detail why an argument was flawed, and then refrained from objecting to the conclusion.

3

John Rawls's Theory of Justice as Fairness

Since it dominates, and provides the springboard for, most contemporary debates about justice, it is essential to have a good grasp of John Rawls's theory of justice. Rawls's *A Theory of Justice* (TJ) was published in 1971, though subsequently revised very mildly in 1999 (all page numbers refer to the revised edition). His subsequent articles and books served to clarify and, in some cases, revise the theory. I shall discuss the theory as it is presented in his final book,[1] *Justice as Fairness: A Restatement* (JF) (2001), because I think this is the simplest, and most authoritative (because most recent), statement of the theory, although I shall refer back both to *A Theory of Justice* and occasionally to other sources where that is important for understanding commonplace objections.

Rawls's purpose is to provide a theory of justice for a free society, in which, he believes, people will have widely differing views about what constitutes a worthwhile life, and what are the correct moral values to live by. He thinks this because he believes that free human reason underdetermines the good: it is just inevitable that reasonable people whose reason is not restrained by a repressive government will disagree profoundly about how best to live their lives. This sets a certain and important limit on what kind of theory he can offer. Whereas it has been common in the history of political philosophy to assume the truth of some particular comprehensive view about what is good in life, and to work out the implications of that view for how political and social life should be governed, Rawls cannot do this. He thinks that an acceptable theory of justice must not depend on moral foundations which are widely disputed among reasonable people. So, for example, John Stuart Mill's version of liberalism rests firmly on the presupposition that utilitarianism is true; but utilitarianism is disputed by reasonable people and thus cannot be the basis of a theory of justice which aims to justify political institutions to reasonable people.

This has important implications for the content of Rawls's theory. In everyday discussions of how much money people should earn, and how much should be redistributed by the state, we commonly appeal to a certain idea of deservingness. We think that people who achieve a great deal deserve to be paid more than people who do not. We think of the great athlete, or the great inventor or successful entrepreneur, as deserving greater rewards than those who are less successful. But Rawls rejects this view. He argues on two grounds. First, he says that we simply do not deserve our place in the distribution of natural endowments:

> This statement is meant as a truism. Who would deny it? Do people really think that they (morally) deserved to be born more gifted than others? Do they think that they morally deserved to be born a man rather than a woman, or vice versa? Do they think that they deserved to be born into a wealthier rather than into a poorer family? No. (JF 74–5)

But if this is true, it makes a mockery of the idea that we could deserve (in the moral sense) to be rewarded for our achievements. If factors which we did not deserve play such a powerful role in explaining our achievements, then the rewards for our achievements must, in large part, be undeserved. In societies with relatively free markets, talent, in particular, is liable to explain a great deal of our success.

One response to this objection to deservingness in the ordinary sense is to make a distinction between the person and the environment he or she inhabits, and say that our talents constitute us as persons; so that although it is true that we do not deserve to have them, given that we have them, we deserve to be rewarded for them. Surely, to say that we cannot be thought of as responsible for them is to alienate us from ourselves? But this response is problematic. First, the environment influences which talents are rewarded, so if we do not deserve to be rewarded for environmental factors, it is going to be hard to justify actual rewards in any particular situation. Two sporting examples will help. Height is an influential quality for success in basketball, that is, most successful basketball players are very tall, because being tall makes it easier to score a basket, which skews the height requirements for other players. Many of the most successful basketball players would not have succeeded in other sports. But whether the most successful player will make a great deal of money depends on how popular basketball is. If it is, as in most countries, a minor and amateur sport, successful players will not make much money. If somebody with the same level of talent is lucky enough to grow up in the United States, where it is extremely popular, they can make a great deal of money. The environment determines how well rewarded the talent will be. And this strategy does not claim that the player deserves his or her environment. Think now about women's tennis. In 1992 Steffi Graff made $1.6 million in tournament winnings, and several times that amount in endorsements and sponsorship agreements. But her earnings in the year following April 1993 were almost double her earnings in 1992. Why? In April 1993 her more successful archrival, Monica Seles, withdrew from the sport, having been stabbed by a deranged 'fan'. The presence or otherwise of Seles in a labour market which rewards coming first had a tremendous impact on the return to Graff's talent. Again, environment is highly influential on reward to talent, and in such a way that we cannot say what the 'true' deserved reward should be.

The second problem with the response is that, on reflection, the talents/environment distinction seems arbitrary when thinking about who we are. Certainly, our personality and character are influenced by the talents we were born with and what we have done with them. But I would still be the person that I am, more or less, if I did not have some of those talents, or had them in lesser or greater abundances. This is easiest to see with talents that one makes relatively little productive use of. I am blessed with extraordinarily good eyesight but, unfortunately, I lack the corresponding aesthetic sensitivity to make good productive use of it. I believe that I would be more or less the same person if I had ordinary eyesight. But I doubt I would be anything like the same person if I had been raised in a radically different environment – say in early medieval Europe or the American Midwest – especially if one of the differences in the environment were that I had been reared by different people from my biological parents.

The second reason why Rawls rejects the ordinary notion of desert as the basis of a theory of justice, however, is that it is widely disputed among reasonable people (in fact, as the quote above suggests, he thinks that no-one really believes it!). Such a view could not serve as the grounds of a theory of justice. We should, Rawls thinks, think of people as deserving whatever it is justice says they should have, rather than thinking of justice as having to give people what they deserve.

The fundamental intuitive ideas

Instead of the concept of desert, Rawls's theory rests on three basic principles which he calls the 'fundamental intuitive ideas'. The three fundamental intuitive ideas are ideas that he thinks are 'implicit' in the fabric of the public political culture of modern democratic societies. In other words they are ideas that are frequently appealed to in political arguments and speeches, or in judicial decisions, or public documents like the US Declaration of Independence and the Universal Declaration of Human Rights. These are the ideas which can serve as the basis of a theory of justice because, unlike our common-sense notion of desert, or Mill's utilitarianism, they can command widespread public agreement.

The first of these fundamental intuitive ideas is the idea of *society as a fair system of cooperation* (TJ 4–6; JF 5–8). This idea has three elements:

1   Cooperation is not mere coordination, but coordination according to rules and procedures accepted by the cooperators as appropriate.

2   Reciprocity/mutuality – the terms are reciprocal in that everyone can reasonably accept them as long as everyone else does so. Notice this avoids the question of what we do when others refuse to abide by the rules.
3   Cooperation is set up to allow the cooperators to advance their own good.

The second is the idea of *a well-ordered society* (TJ 4, 397–405; JF 8–10). A society is well ordered in so far as (a) it fulfils the *publicity condition*, in that everyone accepts and everyone knows that everyone else accepts the same principles of justice, and this knowledge is mutually recognized as if as a matter of public agreement; (b) society's basic structure is known by all to fulfil the requirements of justice; and (c) citizens have an effective sense of justice – they can understand justice and do not rebel against the situation to which it assigns them. Another way of putting this is that they 'know their place'.

The third, and most important, idea is the idea of *citizens as free and equal moral persons* (JF 18–24; TJ 11–12). Citizens are considered to be equal in so far as they:

(a)   have a capacity for a sense of justice and
(b)   have a capacity for a conception of the good – that is, a capacity to hold, revise and rationally pursue a conception of what makes life good.

What is the capacity for a sense of justice? It is the capacity to order one's own behaviour so that it observes the limits described by the legitimate interests of other people. To give a couple of prosaic examples: when you refrain from cheating on a test, or from stealing a newspaper, even though you are pretty sure you could get away with it, you are displaying, in a very crude way, a developed sense of justice, because you are allowing the interests of other people to limit the extent to which you pursue your own self-interest. A sense of justice does not require heroic behaviour, at least when social institutions are not, themselves, radically unjust.

What is the capacity for a conception of the good? Rawls calls the conception of the good a 'rational plan of life' (TJ 358–73), but he is very deliberately non-judgemental about what counts as one. So, for example, Christianity exalts the monastic life, but also the life of a good parent raising a family, whereas Jainism indicates that a life can only be good if it involves consumption of the absolute minimum needed for subsistence. Rawls would count any of these as conceptions of the good, and, to illustrate just how broad a category 'conception of the good' is, he explicitly includes the example of a person whose goal in life is to count out, individually, every single blade of grass on their lawn. This is an unlikely conception of the good, but a conception nevertheless. Notice, though, that the capacity for a conception of the good is not restricted to the capacity to pursue that conception: it includes the capacity to revise it, that is, to think about it in the light of alternatives and, crucially, to change it if there are good reasons to do so. A person who could not reflect on her conceptions of the good, or who found herself unable to it even though she saw good reasons to do so, would, if you like, be addicted to it: she would not have a fully developed capacity for a conception of the good.

Citizens are considered free in so far as they:

(a) regard themselves as self-authenticating sources of claims on society; and
(b) have a right to see themselves as independent of their actual conception of the good.

The idea that we see ourselves as self-authenticating sources of claims on society is fairly straightforward: we see ourselves as entitled to pursue our view of the good life, albeit within the limits set by justice, and we think that the design of social institutions ought to take us into account as individuals. This does not mean that we are purely self-interested, either in our behaviour or in our self-conception: our behaviour is limited by justice, and our self-conception may well, and normally will, involve reference to the interests of others, especially those we care for. The claim is just that we are not entirely self-effacing; we are not servile to the demands and interests of others.

The idea of having a right to see ourselves as independent of our actual conception of the good is more obscure, and can best be understood by thinking about the idea of responsibility. We think of ourselves as persisting through changes in our conception of the good: even though we have changed, or might in the future change, our religion, for example, we think we are still entitled to be treated the same way by society, and that our past praiseworthy and blameworthy acts remain truly ours: society should not release us from jail, or withdraw some honour from us, just because we have changed our view.

The Basic Structure

There is one more preliminary matter to consider before looking at how Rawls justifies his principles, and that is what he regards as the *subject* of justice. The principles of justice apply to what Rawls calls the 'Basic Structure' of society. This consists of some of the central, interaction-shaping institutions of a society: for example, the constitution, the legally recognized forms of property, the structure of the economy, the design of the parliament, and the judiciary. The idea is that these institutions govern the division of the advantages which accrue from social cooperation, and they assign the basic rights and responsibilities to citizens. So a society is just when those institutions are arranged according to the correct principles. Some institutions are not within the Basic Structure. For example, Rawls treats churches (as long as they are not established churches) as being independent of the Basic Structure, and therefore exempt from some of the rules that, for example, would have to be enforced in public institutions. On Rawls's theory it would be unjust for the government to deprive women of the right to vote or to disallow them from being employed in certain professions; but it is permissible for a church to discriminate against women, as long as it makes clear to them that they are free to leave.

Rawls focuses on the Basic Structure for two reasons. First, it is a public coercive institution which operates according to rules; and we are morally bound to justify these rules to one another. When the Basic Structure coerces someone, we are all implicated in that coercion, and need to be able to offer good reasons for it (JF 52–3). Second, the Basic Structure has a profound influence on people's life prospects (JF 10, 55). How well someone fares in life depends in significant part on their place in the Basic Structure and on the way that the Basic Structure is regulated. The easiest way of seeing this is by comparing people's prospects *across* societies. In the United States, for example, if you are born into a household in the lowest decile of income-earners, you are less likely to survive to adulthood than if you are born into that same decile in Norway or Germany. Similarly, if born in Norway, you are many times less likely to spend a substantial part of your life in absolute poverty (defined as 30 per cent of US median income or below) than if you are born in the slightly richer United States. This is not because poor Norwegians are harder-working or more talented than poor Americans; it is because the Basic Structure is differently arranged. So the Basic Structure has a profound influence over people's prospects in life, and is coercive in a way that we need to justify to each other.

The idea of the Basic Structure as the subject of justice corresponds very roughly to the traditional distinction in liberal theory between the public and the private spheres. The idea is that the principles we choose will directly regulate the basic structure, but not the 'private' sphere. It is the basic institutions which have to meet whatever the principles of justice are. As individuals, we are not bound by the principles in our everyday lives (except in so far as we must contribute to maintaining public institutions that meet the principles). This is important, because it illustrates that the goal of the theory is not to tell us how to behave in our personal lives, but to generate principles for establishing a framework within which each of us conducts our behaviour.

The traditional distinction between the public and private spheres has been subjected to much criticism. One of the most common criticisms is that traditionally the private has been treated as beyond criticism, and as if it has no implications for the public sphere, whereas, of course, much private behaviour is reprehensible, and, does indeed have effects on the public sphere. Rawls recognizes this, and is very clear that, although the principles of justice apply directly only to the Basic Structure, the Basic Structure in turn sets constraints on private associations. The Basic Structure may allow churches to excommunicate heretics, but it must forbid them from burning them. It may allow parents to ground their children, but it must forbid them from raping them. It may allow a firm to pay its executives fifteen times the salary of the average worker, but then tax it away disproportionally. The private sphere does not describe some geographical, or personal, space within which people can do whatever they like. Instead, it describes a range of possible decisions which must be left unconstrained, even though we know that people's inclinations will be shaped by the public framework.

The question for Rawls, then, is the following: 'Viewing society as a fair system of cooperation between citizens regarded as free and equal, what principles of justice are most appropriate to specify basic rights and liberties, and to regulate social and economic inequalities in citizens' prospects over a complete life?' (JF 41, see also 39).

The Original Position

So now we get to the lynchpin idea of the theory of justice, which is the idea of the Original Position. The OP is a thought experiment which enables us to work out the consequences of the fundamental intuitive ideas for the design of social institutions. Rawls says that the purpose is to 'make vivid to ourselves the restrictions which it seems reasonable to place on arguments for principles of justice, and therefore on those principles themselves' (JF 18).

Rawls's theory is a development within what is usually known as the social contract tradition. This tradition represents justice in social arrangements as a matter of agreement between the individuals who participate in them. Some contract theorists have thought that in order to be acceptable they have actually to be agreed to by the members of society. But most modern contract theorists do not think that contracts have to be actual. For them, the point of the contract is to represent a moral idea about the relationship between members of society. Before the contract tradition was developed it was common for theorists (and ordinary people) to think that society was properly organized according to some pre-existing moral hierarchy: we owed allegiance to the King, or to the Pope, or to God, and our role in society was determined by our duty to that authority figure, and this debt was rooted not in our personal interests or agreement, but in the fundamental superiority of the authority figure. The idea of a social contract represents the contrary idea that *all members of society are sovereign individuals who are bound to share their sovereignty by their obligations to one another (not to some superior authority)*. They are, in some sense, equals, who merit equal consideration in the design of social institutions.

So, for Rawls, the answer to the question of what count as fair terms of cooperation is best understood as specified by an agreement among the participants in social cooperation themselves. What would free and equal persons agree to under certain specified conditions?

Which conditions? A second important point to note about the contract tradition is that contracts are only morally binding under very specific conditions. For example, if you agree to sell your house to someone who has kidnapped your daughter and is threatening to cut off her ear if you do not sell, that contract is neither morally nor legally binding, because it was made under illegitimate coercion. Contracts are invalidated by being made in illegitimate background conditions. The law usually uses a two-pronged standard for this: it says that fraud and coercion nullify contracts, but allows for many other kinds of conditions, such as asymmetric information and unequal bargaining power, to influence contracts, as long as the beneficiary of the contract is not culpably responsible for these inequalities.

There are good pragmatic reasons for allowing such inequalities to influence contracts between people in the real world. But deciding what principles should govern society is, in Rawls's word, a 'grave' choice. Whereas ordinary contracts are entered into voluntarily, society is entered into without choice: we enter through birth and leave, usually, only by dying. Furthermore, these ordinary contracts will be framed by the Basic Structure – so whatever advantages are allowed to influence the principles will influence the ordinary contracts twice over: first, by influencing the principles, and, second, by influencing the contracts. Rawls therefore seeks to exclude all 'morally arbitrary bargaining advantages' from influencing the choice of principles. He does this by imposing what he calls a *veil of ignorance* on the choosers (ourselves), depriving them of knowledge that would give them bargaining advantage for which there is no moral justification (JF 85–9, especially 82; TJ 118–23). The veil of ignorance *masks* knowledge of our generational membership, our natural endowments, our social class background, and our specific conception of the good (JF 15–16, 86).

The veil of ignorance simultaneously fulfils three functions. Most centrally it models the idea that the principles should be impartial, by ensuring that the parties in the Original Position cannot try to get the principles to favour their own clients. It prevents the well-born, the talented, the physically attractive, from designing the principles specifically to reward their assets. Relatedly, the second function is that it deprives the parties of unequal threat advantage. Assume, for example, that a party knows that she is from an advantaged social class background. Then she might be inclined, because of that, to favour a system with strong rights to private schooling, or strong protections of inheritance against taxes. Depriving her of that knowledge ensures that she will not hold out for a better deal just because she knows that she would thrive without a cooperative arrangement, enjoying, as she does, lots of advantages. It is worth mentioning, though, that the veil is not aimed at ensuring that the principles do not allow the advantaged to get benefits. It is intended to make sure that whatever outcomes are allowed by the principles, there are good impartial reasons for them. So the parties might, in principle, agree to a bar on inheritance taxes, but they will not do so either because some of them feel it will benefit them over others, or because some of them have a better fall-back position than others.

The third function of the veil of ignorance is contributing to the way that the OP models the fundamental intuitive ideas (JF 80–1). So, for example, depriving the parties of knowledge of their conception of the good ensures that they do not try to design the principles to favour their own conception of the good over others. This models impartiality – the idea that it is wrong for the principles of justice to favour, say, Christians over Muslims – but it also models the idea of citizens as free persons who are not essentially tied to their particular conception of the good: the idea that citizens are responsible for their own ends, plans of life, and should not be advantaged or disadvantaged in terms of the distribution of goods by reference to the content of their conceptions. Similarly, depriving us of knowledge of our natural endowments and social class background models the idea of citizens as equal moral persons: what is significant is the fact that we equally have the capacity for a sense of justice and a conception of the good to the minimal requisite degree. That we are unequal in other ways is morally arbitrary and not therefore permitted to enter the design of social institutions.

The veil of ignorance cannot, of course, deprive the parties in the OP of all knowledge. In fact the parties know things that real people don't. The veil of ignorance *reveals* general facts about sociology, history, economics, psychology and the other relevant sciences. This stipulation is very important: it reveals Rawls's commitment to the idea articulated in chapter 2 that the principles of justice must be sensitive to the facts about human nature and about the feasibility of different institutions – his version of the idea that ought implies can. The parties also know that the circumstances of justice hold: that is, that it is a realistic possibility that social cooperation will generate surplus and hence benefits for all but that resources are sufficiently scarce that, given the conceptions of the good which people actually hold in the society, there is liable to be conflict over the distribution of that surplus (JF 84–5). The parties also have whatever other relevant information does not stand in the way of agreement.

The final question that we need to look at is the motivation of the parties in the Original Position. First, Rawls stipulates that the parties pursue only the interests of their clients, who are motivated neither by envy nor by altruism (JF 87). This is a worst case kind of reasoning. If they are altruistic, it might be too easy to get agreement. If we can get agreement when they are self-interested, it should be more achievable when they are not.

Second, in any kind of bargaining we have a level of risk aversion which we bring to it. The outcome of a bargain is bound to be influenced by how risk-averse each of the parties is. When a risk-taker bargains with someone who is risk-averse, under conditions of uncertainty, the outcome is likely to be different than when the bargain is struck between two risk-takers or between two risk-avoiders. This is a problem for the Original Position because a risk-taker might be willing to accept principles which allow for dramatic levels of inequality, on the slight chance that he would be a winner, while a risk-averter might insist on equal outcomes, so as to ensure that she will be safe. So unless there is a fixed level of risk aversion, there are no determinate principles.

Rawls settles the level of risk aversion by what he calls the 'maximin rule' (JF 97–9). This rule guides the agent to look at the full set of scenarios, and to choose the available scenario in which the worst outcome is better than any of the others. This is supposed to be the best guarantee, in the admittedly unusual bargaining circumstances of the OP, of ensuring that the person has a position which is acceptable to them.

Some commentators object to this extraordinarily high level of risk aversion, since in our normal lives even the most timid of us rarely use the maximin rule. But Rawls places great stress on the gravity of the choice facing the parties, and it is this gravity which is supposed to justify the maximin decision rule. The clients and their progeny must expect to live in perpetuity with the choice of principles made (JF 98).

This is a good illustration of the way that the OP models the fundamental intuitive ideas. Remember that the idea of a well-ordered society includes the idea that citizens should have an effective sense of justice: that is, that they can, among other things, live with the situation to which justice assigns them. And remember that the parties in the OP stand in something like an attorney/client relation to the citizens of a well-ordered society. In other words, they are trustees for the interests of their clients, and don't know their conceptions of the good or levels of risk aversion; but they do know that they will have no way out of the basic structure which is selected (JF 98).

A different objection to the high level of risk aversion may, however, have more power. Does assuming that the parties need to ensure that their result is one that their clients could live with really generate the maximin rule, as Rawls suggests?

Rawls rests the case for using the maximin rule on the gravity of the choice, and in most grave-choice situations that may be reasonable, if our aim is to ensure that the worst possible outcome is one that the client can live with. But the Original Position has an unusual feature, which is that the choice in the OP is not urgent. Because the OP takes place outside of time and space, as it were, the parties have the leisure to consider and explore every conceivable principle. Why, then, should they not use the decision rule most naturally suggested by the fact that they need to ensure that their clients can live with whatever outcome they face: the so-called 'satis-min rule'? Satis-min simply directs the agent to seek a satisfactory worst possible outcome: so it would restrict the parties to selecting the set of basic structures in which the worst off people are satisfactorily well off, but would not guide further choice among them.

I want to head off two obvious, and common, objections. The first is that people cannot imagine themselves behind a veil of ignorance, so they are being asked to do the impossible. This is true but irrelevant. Rawls is not asking us actually to imagine ourselves behind a veil of ignorance. He is asking us what people who were behind a veil of ignorance would agree to. His later way of posing the situation, which distinguishes the parties in the Original Position from the persons to whom the agreement will apply, makes it much easier to imagine.

The second objection is that the Original Position describes a hypothetical bargaining situation, and hypothetical contracts, unlike actual ones, give us no reason to act. Just because we *would have* agreed to something in the Original Position, why should we act on it *now*? How can a theory of justice arrived at in such a way have binding force? In answering this, it is important to remember that for Rawls what the Original Position does is help us to draw out the consequences for how to think about justice of more fundamental moral ideas which, he thinks, we already accept or which, if we do not, can be justified independently. So, for Rawls, showing that we would have agreed to something in the Original Position is tantamount to showing that there are good impartial reasons for believing it. The fact that we would have agreed to it has no independent bearing on whether we should accept it. The reason that we should accept it is that there are good reasons to accept it, which the discussion of the OP demonstrates.

The parties in the Original Position compare rival principles of justice, considering whether they will be able to justify their selection of the principles to their clients. Although the parties are, officially, bargaining with each other, the deliberations do not have an adversarial flavour, because the parties have exactly the same responsibilities toward their clients, each of whom has, as far as the parties now, exactly the same interests. They know that if they all reason accurately they will all support as their first best choice the same principles, so the deliberations are, to all intents and purposes, collaborative.

Two questions have to be settled. What are the goods that the parties pursue? And how will those goods be distributed – what, if you like, is the correct distributive rule?

In ordinary bargaining situations the parties dispute the distribution of the things they really care about. However, the veil of ignorance prevents the parties in the Original Position from doing this, because they do not know their actual conceptions of the good – they do not know, in other words, what they really care about. So Rawls needs to provide them with reasons to care about something. He does this by describing what he calls a 'thin theory of the good' – a theory of primary goods, which are goods that people would have reason to care about having regardless of whatever else they had reason to care about. In his later writings Rawls supplements this account of the primary goods by connecting them to the fundamental intuitive idea of free and equal persons. The primary goods are goods that citizens have reason to want given their interest in exercising and developing their capacities for a conception of the good and for a sense of justice (JF 62, 91–4). The primary goods fall into three categories (JF 57–60):

(a)   *natural primary goods*: health, intelligence, talents, limbs, eyesight, and so on – these are *not* (according to Rawls) available for distribution;
(b)   *social primary goods* (see below) – these *are* available for distribution; and

(c) *self-respect* – this depends in part on the distribution of social primary goods, but is not distributed itself.

The natural primary goods are the natural endowments of individuals. As such, according to Rawls, they may not be redistributed. There is remarkably little debate about whether they should be distributed, though some theorists, as we shall see, do think that they should count in the determination of how well off people are from the point of view of justice. It is not clear that Rawls disagrees with this, but it is striking that he feels entitled to neglect the question because he develops his theory under a simplifying assumption that I have not yet mentioned. He says that:

> Our aim is to ascertain the conception of justice appropriate for a democratic society in which citizens conceive of themselves in a certain way. So let's add that all citizens are fully cooperating members of society over the course of a complete life. This means that everyone has sufficient intellectual powers to play a normal part in society, and no-one suffers from unusual needs that are especially difficult to fulfil, for example, unusual and costly medical requirements. . . . At this initial stage the fundamental problem of justice arises between those who are full and active and morally conscientious participants in society. (Rawls 1980: 545–6; see also JF 20, 168–9)

In other words, no-one is severely and chronically disabled. So, the question of redistributing natural primary goods does not arise.

This is not the place to defend Rawls's neglect of disabilities, though we shall discuss it briefly in chapter 4. But Rawls's own defence is that this is a form of best case reasoning. If it turned out that his theory of justice could not work, even for this best case, then we could confidently assume that it would not work for more difficult and complex cases, and so could reject it.

The social primary goods *are* available for redistribution, and are as follows:

1 The basic liberties (freedom of thought and liberty of conscience, etc.) are the background institutions necessary for

the development and exercise of the capacity to decide upon and revise, and rationally pursue, a conception of the good. Similarly, these liberties allow for the development and exercise of the sense of right and justice under political and social conditions that are free.

2   Freedom of movement and free choice of occupation against a background of diverse opportunities are required for the pursuit of final ends as well as to give effect to a decision to revise and change them, if one so desires.

3   Powers and prerogatives of offices of responsibility are needed to give scope to various self-governing and social capacities of the self.

4   Income and wealth, understood broadly as they must be, are all-purpose means (having a exchange value) for achieving directly or indirectly a wide range of ends, whatever they happen to be.

5   The social basis of self-respect is those aspects of basic institutions that are normally essential if citizens are to have a lively sense of their own worth as moral persons and to be able to realize their highest-order interests and advance their ends with self-confidence.

The two principles

How are the social primary goods to be distributed? Rawls's theory of justice is constituted by his two principles of justice, and two priority rules (JF 42–3).

The First Principle
Each person has the same indefeasible claim to a fully adequate scheme of equal basic liberties, which scheme is compatible with the same scheme of liberties for all.

The Second Principle
Social and economic inequalities are to satisfy two conditions: first, they are to be attached to offices and positions open to all under conditions of fair equality of opportunity; and, second, they are to be to the greatest benefit of the least advantaged.

I shall explain exactly what the principles mean as we look at the arguments for them. The two priority rules are as follows. The first principle has what Rawls calls *lexical priority* over the second principle. This means that nothing may be done to implement the second principle which violates, or jeopardizes, the first principle. When the second principle conflicts with the first, in other words, the first always wins out. The second priority rule is that the first condition specified in the second rule has lexical priority over the second condition. What this means is that inequalities which benefit the least advantaged are only acceptable as long as the competition for them is arranged under conditions of fair equality of opportunity.

The principles can be broken down, then, into the following rules:

1   The basic liberties are distributed equally.
2   Opportunities to access the powers and prerogatives of office and the unequal material rewards attached to office are distributed equally (among those with similar levels of talent and willingness to exert effort, about which more later), as far as is consistent with the Liberty Principle.
3   Income and wealth is distributed to the greatest benefit of those who have least, as far as is consistent with the Liberty Principle and the principle of fair equality of opportunity.

The second principle

In discussing the arguments for the principles, I'll work backwards, starting with the second. We've seen that it comes in two parts:

1   Any inequalities must be to the benefit of the least advantaged.
2   Any inequalities must be attached to offices and positions open to all under fair equality of opportunity.

When Rawls introduces the second principle he first presents a general conception, which is much vaguer than the more refined statement above. He says that 'social and economic inequalities are to be arranged so that they are both (a) reasonably expected to be to *everyone's advantage*, and (b) attached to positions and offices *open to all* (TJ 66). However, as he notes, the two phrases that I have emphasized here are ambiguous, and so need to be refined. He presents the first intuitive argument for the second principle through a discussion in which he disambiguates, or refines, these two phrases. Of course, this is not a fundamental argument for the second principle, since it does not give reasons for accepting the general conception, and it is furthermore not the kind of argument that would be admissible in the Original Position, appealing as it does to substantive moral considerations rather than the self-interest of the parties. It is instructive nevertheless. Rawls takes us through two possible interpretations of each of the ambiguous phrases, and three of the possible combinations of those interpretations.

The first combination is what he calls the 'natural liberty' version of the second principle, in which 'everyone's advantage' is interpreted as meaning 'efficiency', and 'open to all' is interpreted as meaning 'careers open to talents' (TJ 58). The principle of 'careers open to talents' states that no-one should be discriminated against at the point of hiring (or being admitted to an educational programme) except on grounds strictly relevant to their likely performance in the position. So it prevents universities and employers from discriminating against female or black applicants for example, but does not require the government to ensure that those applicants have had equal educational opportunities prior to the time of being selected for university or hired for the position. Rawls understands efficiency as a technical notion: an allocation is efficient when any change in the allocation could not make anyone better off without making someone worse off.

What's wrong with the natural liberty version of the second principle? The problem according to Rawls is that although there is formal equality of opportunity, there is no 'effort to preserve an equality, or similarity of social conditions', and so 'the initial distribution of assets for any period of time is strongly influenced by natural and social contingencies' (TJ 62), and the influence of these contingencies will be allowed to accumulate over generations. So, for example, someone who is talented and well born will be well rewarded, which will enable him to buy for his less talented child an expensive education which will enable him to do better than an equally talented but less well-born child in the competition for positions and the incomes attached to them. Over time, the problem is that 'distributive shares [are permitted to be] influenced improperly by factors which are arbitrary from the moral point of view' (TJ 63, see also JF 43).

So Rawls turns to the Liberal version of the second principle (JF 43–4; TJ 63–4), which continues to interpret everyone's advantage as efficiency, but interprets 'open to all' as what he calls 'fair equality of opportunity'. In careers open to talents we focus only on the positions themselves. We say: well, what matters is that when two people are up for the same job, the one whose talents most suit her to it should get it. This is, of course, a great progress over historical methods of allocation – for example, by birth. Previously many people were excluded from many positions regardless of the talent they might have revealed for those positions. Careers open to talents prevents this, but it still does not prevent the more talented, hard-working people from failing to get the jobs to which they are most suited. Fair equality of opportunity is aimed at preventing this, and also presents a serious barrier to the accumulation of advantage over generations because it says that people with similar levels of talent and willingness to exert effort should face similar prospects for success regardless of their social class of origin: 'in all parts of society there are to be roughly the same prospects of culture and achievement for those similarly motivated and endowed' (JF 44). This is quite a demanding criterion. If it were to be completely fulfilled, social class background would have no influence at all over someone's expectations in life: something which no known society has achieved. Of course, it is important to note that any interpretation of the second principle operates only under the constraints imposed by the priority of the first principle. So it may well be that when fully fair equality of opportunity is up and running, people who are similarly talented and willing to exert effort will face unequal prospects, but this would be because the Liberty Principle prohibits certain of the measures that would be needed to achieve fully fair equality of opportunity. The principle itself is extremely radical. It does not restrict its attention to the hiring process but extends that focus to the social background conditions, so that only differences in talent and effort may alter outcomes.

Rawls takes pains to emphasize that efficiency plays no role in motivating the adoption of fair equality of opportunity. It may well result in a more efficient allocation of human capital, but that is not the reason for it. Suppose we found some characteristic, let's say having blue eyes, which correlated almost but not quite perfectly with low IQ. It might be extremely costly to identify the paltry number of blue-eyed people with average to high IQs, so expensive that it would be more efficient simply to treat all blue-eyed people as having low IQs. This would not, according to Rawls, justify doing so, because to do so would assault the dignity of those few within the group who have the average to high IQs. This value – dignity – trumps the value of efficiency.

Fair equality of opportunity remains as part of the version of the second principle that Rawls ultimately endorses, so before moving on to look at the problems with the Liberal version of the second principle, we should ask whether there is an argument for fair equality of opportunity from within the original position. At least two pertinent considerations are available to the parties in the original position. First, they know what is suggested above, that it is extremely injurious to an individual's dignity if she knows that another has more chance of getting some benefit as a result of the design of social institutions, but that there is no (morally justifiable) reason for that inequality. This is most obvious in cases of discrimination at the point of hiring: when a black American knows that she was denied a position which went to a white solely because the white was white, that fact assaults her dignity more than if she knows that she lost out because her rival was likely to be better at the job. But it is also striking in cases which are not ruled out by careers open to talents. For example, if two people with similar levels of talent and willingness to exert effort apply for a university place, and the losing candidate has reason to believe that the winning candidate's admission was due to her superior schooling up to that point, she is likely to feel her dignity assaulted. Whenever we see our prospects undermined for reasons over which we have had no control, we are degraded. This appears to be the primary consideration at work.

The second consideration apparently available to the parties in the Original Position concerns the structure of the opportunity space. It may appear that opportunities, unlike income and wealth, are zero-sum goods, so that distributing them unequally does not give more to those who have least, as, for example, distributing income and wealth unequally might benefit those who have least (as I shall suggest below). It might be objected that making opportunities equal might make everyone worse off, because people who are productive will make better use of productive opportunities than people who are less productive. But this objection fits well with what fair equality of opportunity actually demands, which is that opportunities among people with similar levels of talent and willingness to exert effort be made equal.

The most explicit defence of fair equality of opportunity that Rawls makes is the following:

> The reasons for requiring open positions are not solely, or even partly, those of efficiency . . . if some places were not open on a fair basis to all, those kept out would be right in feeling unjustly treated even though they benefit from the greater efforts of those who were allowed to exercise them. They would be justified in their complaint not only because they were excluded from certain external rewards of office such as wealth and privilege, but because they were debarred from the experience of the realization of self which comes from a skilful and devoted exercise of social duties. They would be deprived of one of the main forms of human good. (TJ 73)

In other words the opportunity to enjoy the particular rewards of certain jobs is so valuable that it cannot be compensated for by, for example, redistributing income and wealth. For someone who wants to be a doctor, or a teacher, and is locked out of that opportunity for morally arbitrary reasons, there is no amount of money that could erase her regret at being denied the opportunity. So, Rawls seems to think, such opportunities should be distributed equally, and this principle is prior to the difference principle.

Although fair equality of opportunity is extremely radical, the Liberal version of the second principle is inadequate, Rawls thinks, for two reasons. First, he says, it does not respond adequately to the moral arbitrariness of the natural lottery: 'within the limits allowed by the background arrangements, distributive shares are decided by the outcome of the natural lottery; and this outcome is arbitrary from a moral perspective. There is no more reason to permit the distribution of income to be settled by the distribution of natural assets than by historical and social fortune' (TJ 64). Second, however, fair equality of opportunity cannot even be fully implemented as long as the family continues to exist (which Rawls never questions that it will), because 'even the willingness to make an effort, to try, and so to be deserving in the ordinary sense is itself dependent on happy family and social circumstances' (TJ 64; see also JF 163).

These problems lead Rawls to endorse the Democratic Equality version of the second principle, which combines the fair equality of opportunity interpretation of 'open to all' with what he calls the Difference Principle – understanding 'everyone's advantage' as 'to the greatest benefit of the least advantaged'.

In fact, efficiency, at least understood in the way that economists tend to understand it, could never be an adequate understanding of 'everyone's advantage' for the purposes of a principle of justice. Efficiency, remember, is understood as Pareto optimality. A situation is Pareto optimal if and only if no transfer can make someone better off without making someone else worse off. But this says nothing about the justice of the initial situation. We need a specification of the circumstances in which judgements of efficiency can have force. So, for example, if one person has all the surplus wealth in a society (that is, everyone else lives precisely at subsistence level), the situation may well be Pareto optimal – it may be impossible to benefit any of the others without making that one person worse off. That fact does not count at all against transferring resources from him to others, however. It is not even a count in its favour, overridden by the counts against it. If we said of such a situation, 'oh well, at least it is efficient', we would be being ironic, possibly at the expense of our economist friends.

So some other interpretation of everyone's advantage is needed. One obvious alternative is equality, especially given the observation that underpins the Original Position, that the distribution of talents is morally arbitrary. In fact, although Rawls rejects this alternative, it is the baseline against which he evaluates other alternatives. Income and wealth, and the other goods for which they are proxies, should be distributed equally, except in so far as an unequal distribution will benefit those who have least.

Why does Rawls reject equality as an interpretation of 'everyone's advantage'? It is useful to make the argument from within the Original Position. Think of yourself as representing a client within the Original Position, bargaining for an outcome that will be acceptable to your client. Think of yourself as considering two principles: strict equality, according to which income and wealth are to be distributed equally at the highest feasible level; and the Difference Principle. Now assume strict equality, and compare how well off your client will be under strict equality with how well off she would have been under the Difference Principle. Under the Difference Principle there are two possibilities for your client: she might have been either among the worst off, or among the group better off than the worst off. But by definition, under the Difference Principle every position is either better off than every position under strict equality, or every position is identical to every position under strict equality. If the former, then whether your client will be among the worst off or some better off group, she would prefer to be living under the Difference Principle than under strict equality. If all the positions are identical, then she will be indifferent between the Difference Principle and strict equality. So she can be worse off under strict equality than under the Difference Principle, and cannot be worse off under the Difference Principle than under strict equality. So you should prefer the Difference Principle (see JF 49, 71).

This argument assumes (what the Original Position assumes) that your client is entirely self-interested: she does not care about how much others get. But imagine now that your client is prepared to sacrifice her own well-being for the sake of others, and then compare the situations. Imagine your client living under strict equality, and contemplating the possibility that she would have been among the more advantaged within a society governed by the Difference Principle. She would have been happy to sacrifice for the sake of other people's well-being. But she can see that she has sacrificed for nobody's benefit – she is worse off than she would have been under the Difference Principle, but everyone else is worse off, or at least nobody is better off, than under the Difference Principle. Her sacrifice is futile.

How does the Difference Principle work? How, in other words, could inequalities benefit the least advantaged, that is, those who have least when there is an inequality? The easiest way to illustrate this is by thinking about income and wealth. If income is distributed equally, then everyone gets the same regardless of how productive they are. If, by contrast, income is distributed unequally according to how productive people are, those who can be more productive have an incentive to be so. In order for them to have an incentive, they must be able to keep some of the extra they produce, but not necessarily all; and the surplus which is unnecessary for the incentive can be redistributed to the benefit of the less productive. Incentives for greater production, and redistribution to the least advantaged, can make the least advantaged better off than under equality (JF 64).

Now, some people are sceptical about the story I have just told, and think that inequalities always leave the least advantaged worse off than they would have been under equality. But they do not, in virtue of that belief, have reason to reject the Difference Principle. The Difference Principle allows inequalities only when they *really do* benefit the least advantaged; if you believe that is never, then you believe that the Difference Principle mandates equality, and have no practical reason for preferring one principle over the other.

But let's assume that the Difference Principle does mandate inequalities. If so, then it still allows morally arbitrary factors to influence reward, since the more talented are more likely to be among the most advantaged and the less talented are more likely to be among the least advantaged. Similarly, it does not overcome the other problem Rawls identifies with the Liberal version of the second principle: as long as children are raised in families, happy family circumstances (which include the family's social class) will influence both their inclination to exert effort, and, independently, their prospects.

So the problems are not with fair equality of opportunity, but with the overall interpretation of the second principle.

The so-called 'Democratic Equality' interpretation adjusts the understanding of *advantage*: that is, it reinterprets the first element so that it does some work correcting for natural contingencies. It understands 'everyone's advantage' as 'the greatest benefit of the least advantaged', that is, as meaning that whoever has least income and wealth has more than they would under any other arrangement. Although morally arbitrary natural contingencies do indeed influence people's prospects when the Difference Principle operates, they do so for a non-arbitrary reason: that the least advantaged are better off than they would be under any other arrangement. The Difference Principle represents 'an agreement to regard the distribution of native endowments as a common asset and to share in the benefits of this distribution whatever it turns out to be' (JF 75). If you like, morally arbitrary factors, although they retain some influence, do so only to the extent that morally acceptable reasons support.

What about Rawls's other problem with the fair equality of opportunity interpretation of 'open to all'? Fair equality of opportunity cannot be fully implemented without the removal of the family, for two reasons: first, because it is going to be impossible fully to compensate for the extra resources children inherit from their wealthier (or more generous, or more capable) parents; and, second, because parenting actually affects children's capacity and inclination to exert effort. Now, one response to this problem might be to abolish the family, and Rawls even asks at one point, in this context, 'is the family to be abolished then?' (TJ 448; see also JF 163). I shall not dwell on this, but Rawls's answer is no, although it is not entirely clear what his reasoning is. However, two obvious answers come to mind. The first is that the right to rear a family, or something like it, is protected by the Liberty Principle (which, in Rawls's theory, is prioritized over fair equality of opportunity). This would be so if the right to rear a family, or to be reared in a family, was essential for the development and exercise of some aspect of the moral powers. The second answer is less principled, but equally compelling: even if we abolished the family, there is no reason to believe that we could devise some other arrangement that would solve the problems. Suppose that children are to be raised in state-run orphanages rather than in families, and that these orphanages are well run (unlike actual orphanages). There is every reason to suppose that in well-run orphanages, in which, if they *are* well run, each child will bond closely with different rearers, some rearers will provide happier upbringings, which better prompt the children to exert effort than others. Similarly, it is hard to believe that, without incredibly intrusive monitoring and regulation, different rearers would not be moved to provide their wards with gifts and resources that are worth more to some children than to others. We simply do not know how fully to overcome the barriers to fair equality of opportunity. But limiting the level of inequality the society exhibits has two relevant effects: it diminishes the inequality of resources that children can inherit from their parents – because household income and wealth are more equal, parents are more equally able to pass on advantages to their children; and it limits the usefulness of those resources that parents can confer on their children for getting access to the unequally distributed benefits of social cooperation, because those benefits are distributed more equally (see Swift 2003 and in press for valuable discussions of the problem of the family).

Within the second principle, as I have said, fair equality of opportunity is accorded a particularly strong form of priority. We shall see shortly that it is not clear quite why Rawls gives it that priority, but for the moment I want to explain what its priority means in practice. Within the constraints set by the Liberty Principle and its priority it means the following:

1   Inequalities of income and wealth that might otherwise be allowed by the Difference Principle (in other words, that would benefit the least advantaged) are ruled out if they would, predictably, have the effect of improving the prospects of children born into more advantaged households relative to those born in least advantaged households.

2   Goods, such as education and healthcare, that strongly impact upon people's prospects in life should be distributed, as far as possible, without regard to family income. So, for example, as far as possible, the government should ensure that wealthy parents cannot buy educational

advantages for their children by opting out of public schools and into private schools, or (as they currently can in the United States) by moving to wealthy communities in which the state spends more money on schooling than in poor communities. And the state should ensure that the quality of healthcare a child receives is not influenced by his or her parents' income, either by making private healthcare unavailable to children, or by providing such a high quality of healthcare publicly that no advantage is gained by 'going private'.

3   It will be necessary to raise whatever taxes on inheritance and gifting are necessary to ensure that the children of the wealthy cannot be unduly advantaged by this means. This is potentially a very demanding condition, because a great deal of the benefit children of wealthy families gain from their parents concerns not the actual money that is given or left to them, but the attitude they are able to take toward risk. Knowing that their parents' wealth can cushion them against failure means that some potentially lucrative activities – opening a restaurant, spending several years in medical, art or drama school, taking a low-paid internship in Washington – simply represent less of a risk for them than they do for children without parental back-up. The child who succeeds financially in one of these activities, and therefore never has to claim their parents' resources, might nevertheless have benefited tremendously from the availability of those resources.

Is there an *independent* argument for fair equality of opportunity and its priority over the difference principle? Its not clear that Rawls every really provides one, and in fact, in a footnote in *Justice as Fairness*, he questions, for the first time, whether fair equality of opportunity really should be given the stringent priority he has always granted it:

> Some think that the lexical priority of fair equality of oppor-tunity over the difference principle is too strong, and that either a weaker priority or a weaker form of the opportunity principle would be better, and indeed more in accord with fun-damental ideas of justice as fairness itself. At present I do not know what is best here, and simply register my uncertainty. (JF 163 fn. 44)

If there is an argument, I think it must be modelled on the argument that Rawls gives for the priority of the Liberty Principle (which we shall encounter later). The parties in the Original Position see the opportunities governed by fair equality of opportunity as prior to, and not exchangeable for, income and wealth because, not knowing their conception of the good, they recognize o portunities as *conditions for the exercise* of their conception of the good, the waiving of which for the sake of *means for their exercise* would be futile. Whether resources are actually means for pursuing a conception of the good depends entirely on whether we have the conditions for using them in pursuit of that conception, so it would be irrational to trade opportunities for resources.

The problem with this argument is that the distinction between means and conditions is not as clear as might at first appear. Means (resources) are themselves conditions for the exercise of a conception of the good, or at least can purchase those conditions. My own position is perhaps a good illustration. Much of what is enjoyable about my own job is the leisure I have to contemplate difficult philosophical questions. Once I have the training to do this, I do not in fact need to have a job as a philosopher, just the leisure time and financial security to do it. In other words I do indeed need the freedom to do it, but I do not need a position doing it, just the financial resources and freedom. A big enough income does indeed substitute for the opportunity to attain a position as a philosopher. Other jobs, it is true, are not all like this. One needs to have both the training and a position as a surgeon, in order to enjoy what is rewarding about being a surgeon. In questioning the above argument I am not suggesting that resources always, or even usually, substitute for opportunities for positions, just that they sometimes do, which is all that is needed to cast doubt on the lexical priority that Rawls gives to fair equality of opportunity.

Justifying the Difference Principle   How might parties in the Original Position arrive at the Difference Principle? Remember that the level of risk aversion all the parties share is set by their status as trustees of the interests of their clients, and by the fact that, because a just society is a well-ordered society, they care a great deal that their clients will be guaranteed a position which is acceptable. In a well-ordered society everyone has an effective sense of justice – that is, they are able to live with the position that justice assigns to them – and this means that a very high priority is placed on ensuring an acceptable worst outcome for the client. So the Original Position (by stipulation) fulfils the very unusual conditions in which the maximin decision rule is an appropriate decision rule: parties are ignorant of the probability that their client will do well or badly within each possible set of outcomes; they care relatively little about how well their clients will do above the acceptable minimum (because as long as the minimum is acceptable, positions above the minimum will be acceptable); and the choice is very grave, because their client will have to live their whole life in the society shaped by the chosen principles (see JF 98–9 for a, frankly rather opaque, discussion of the maximin rule, or TJ 132–4 for a clearer presentation).

Although I have been discussing the principles as if each component is argued for separately, that is not technically what occurs in the Original Position. The parties compare rival principles and sets of principles *en bloc*, and choose the set of ordered principles that does best. So justice as fairness is, in fact, proposed and considered as an organized package. Still, it is instructive to look at the motivation for each element of the package, and, given the maximin decision rule, and assuming that the Liberty Principle and fair equality of opportunity are fixed and given priority, it is not hard to see the motivation for the Difference Principle within the Original Position. Each person will have an equal set of liberties, and will enjoy fair equality of opportunity. The parties are fixated, then, on the worst position their client might have to endure, which, in each set of outcomes, is the worst position. So they want to do their best to ensure that the worst outcome will be acceptable to their client, and the way to do this is to make sure that the outcome is as good as possible: to maximize the minimum outcome, or to arrange the system to the greatest benefit of the least advantaged. This is what justifies the Difference Principle.

I've already discussed and deflated one possible objection to the Difference Principle, the egalitarian objection based on scepticism that inequalities can ever benefit the least advantaged, and in chapter 8 I shall indirectly discuss a more sophisticated egalitarian objection. More common are inegalitarian objections. I shall address just one here, and leave others till chapter 5, which considers a series of arguments against redistributive taxation. The current objection concerns Rawls's comment that the Difference Principle represents 'an agreement to regard the distribution of native endowments as a common asset and to share in the benefits of this distribution whatever it turns out to be' (JF 75). This comment is sometimes said to show that the Difference Principle violates our rights to self-ownership (Nozick 1974: 214–15). After all, we own our natural talents, and no-one else has a right to them, and if the Difference Principle denies this, then it is denying us one of our fundamental human rights. If our talents are common property, what is there, in principle, that prevents a government with the necessary technology from redistributing them? Why, for example, shouldn't a technologically advanced government be permitted forcibly to redistribute eyes from the sighted to the blind?

This objection is based on a misreading of the sentence I have quoted. Rawls does not assert that *our talents* are common assets, but that *their distribution* is regarded as a common asset. So our individual talents belong to us individually, and are inalienable in the strongest possible sense; but we regard their distribution as something that we take advantage of for the sake of all. We think of individuals as being fortunate to have the talents they do, but do not think that there is some standard demanding that particular talents deserve particular rewards independently of the value they produce for others. In fact many advocates of 'free' markets (like, for example, Adam Smith) seem to have a similar view: they say that markets have the wonderful feature that they give individuals self-interested incentives to exercise their talents in ways that benefit others. Consider Michael Jordan. Jordan was an outstanding basketball player and, let's assume (perhaps unfairly), had no other unusual talents, so that his career choices were between basketball and some average-paying job. According to advocates of free markets, he did not deserve to be paid well simply because he was an outstanding basketball player who played a lot of basketball. If no-one were interested in paying to watch him, there would be no reason at all for him to be rewarded. In a culture in which people have no interest in basketball, basketball players would be paid no more than people in other jobs, and there is nothing wrong with that. Constructing free markets amounts to an agreement to treat the distribution of talents as a common asset just as much as does implementing the Difference Principle. The difference between them is that the Difference Principle realizes a particular conception of the 'common': one which prioritizes the benefit to the least advantaged.

The Liberty Principle

Finally, let's turn to the first principle, the Liberty Principle. Here it is again:

Each person has the same indefeasible claim to a fully adequate scheme of equal basic liberties, which scheme is compatible with the same scheme of liberties for all.

What constitutes a fully adequate scheme of basic liberties? Rawls draws up the list of basic liberties in the same way that he does the other social primary goods: by looking at the essential political and social conditions required for the adequate development and full exercise of the two moral powers of citizens regarded as free and equal moral persons. In other words he asks what conditions are necessary for the development and exercise of the two moral powers: our capacities for a sense of justice and for a conception of the good. He distinguishes three cases, each of which justifies particular liberties.

1 Free and equal citizens have a capacity for a sense of justice and an interest in exercising it. This justifies the political liberties and right to freedom of thought, and some rights to freedom of expression.
2 Our interest in developing and exercising our capacity for a conception of the good yields liberty of conscience, religious freedom, freedom of movement and of association, and a right to privacy.
3 (Subsidiary case.) There are freedoms which service the above ones: (ancillary) liberties associated with the

physical and psychological integrity of the person, rights covered by the rule of law, due process, and so on (Rawls 1992: 332–3; JF 45).

Rawls's method of drawing up the list of basic liberties helps solve what would otherwise be a serious problem: how to work out the relative significance of different liberties. In chapter 5 we shall see how difficult it is for libertarians to justify strong rights in private property by appeal to the value of liberty or freedom, and that this is because they use an undifferentiated conception of freedom as 'the absence of coercion by our fellow man'. If we drew up the list of liberties by appeal to this conception of freedom, it would be impossible to say anything satisfactory about the relative importance of different liberties. Restrictions that prevent us from driving the wrong way up a one-way street are just as much restrictions on our liberty (in this sense) as are restrictions that prohibit us from speaking up in support of terrorist activities, and they are, for most of us, far more restrictive, since they prevent us from doing something we actually might want to do. They are, nevertheless, entirely acceptable, while the prohibition against free speech for supporters of terrorism is unacceptable. Why? Not, certainly, because one involves more coercion than the other. Rawls's method, by contrast, gives us a principled way of answering the question. We can see that freedom of expression and the correlative freedom to hear the expression of others contributes to our exercise and development of our capacities for a conception of the good and a sense of justice; the freedom to drive the wrong way down a one-way street does not. It also helps us to work out the content of particular basic liberties. The right to freedom of expression, for example, does not protect someone's right maliciously to shout 'Fire!' in a (non-burning) crowded theatre, and it allows for mild punishment of libel and defamation, because such acts of expression do not (usually) serve the pertinent interests.

What is the argument for the Liberty Principle and its priority over the second principle? A fairly straightforward argument is available within the Original Position for both the Liberty Principle and granting it some sort of priority (though not necessarily the lexical priority Rawls claims for it). The parties in the Original Position, remember, are ignorant of their clients' conception of the good, and are concerned to ensure an acceptable position for their clients. They know that to live in a society in which one could not pursue one's conception of the good, and revise it in the light of reason and experience, would be unacceptable, so they know that their clients have a very powerful interest in having the basic conditions needed for pursuit and rational revision of their conception of the good – basic liberties. In *A Theory of Justice* and *Justice as Fairness* Rawls makes a version of this argument in support of one particular liberty, the basic liberty of freedom of conscience. He explains that the parties in the Original Position do know that their clients will have moral and religious commitments which will specify various obligations, but they know neither what those commitments will be nor how widely they will be shared in the society they will inhabit. So any principle which put in jeopardy the conditions for them being able to affirm and carry out the obligations specified by their conception of the good would be unacceptable if an alternative principle was available that guaranteed those conditions. But such a principle is available: the principle that all should have liberty of conscience (TJ 181–2; JF 104–5). So the parties would adopt it as an element of the package of principles they select overall.

Similar reasoning probably supports most of the other basic liberties: they constitute conditions for the exercise and development of our capacities for a conception of the good and a sense of justice, and the veil of ignorance ensures that they cannot simply secure liberty for their clients' own conception of the good without simultaneously securing it for others, and this affects the choices they will make concerning freedom of expression, freedom of association, and even the political liberties.

This is not yet any sort of argument that the Liberty Principle should have priority, let alone lexical priority, over the second principle of justice. Rawls does make such an argument, but, as we shall see, it is problematic. First, let's get clear on what the priority of the Liberty Principle amounts to. It means that nothing may be done to implement either fair equality of opportunity or maximin that would compromise the Liberty Principle, or, to put it another way, that would infringe any of the basic liberties. So if an inequality arises from someone's legitimate exercise of a basic liberty, even if that inequality is not to the benefit of the least advantaged, it must be permitted. Similarly, though, even if an inequality would be to the greatest benefit of the least advantaged, it is not permitted if a basic liberty must be infringed to produce it.

Why should the Liberty Principle have this sort of priority? Think about the argument above: what if you were willing to give up some part of your freedom of conscience in return for, say, more income? Suppose that the part of freedom of conscience you had given up was the part necessary to allow you to carry out practices vital to your conception of the good. How would you have gained? According to Rawls, not at all: the extra income simply isn't worth anything because you cannot do with it what you want to do with it. So the appearance of there having been a real exchange is misleading: you have gained nothing and lost your liberty.

Rawls does make another comment about the priority of the Liberty Principle. He says that 'the basic liberties protect fundamental interests that have a special significance. This distinctive feature is connected with the often intractable nature of religious, philosophical and moral conflicts in the absence of a secure public basis of mutual trust' (JF 105). In other words, as I understand it, the Liberty Principle must have a special kind of security because infringements of basic liberties will always threaten the public basis of trust necessary for a just state to reproduce itself over time.

Radical critics of liberalism have sometimes pressed a distinction between formal and substantive freedom. Formal freedom is merely freedom from interference by other human agents. But having the formal freedom to do something does not mean that one can actually do it; one also needs the means to do it. The starving man has the formal freedom to eat, but not the substantive freedom (for a valuable discussion that problematizes this distinction, see Swift 2001: 53–4). Rawls himself draws a parallel distinction between the equal liberties and their value or worth: 'Liberty is represented by the complete system of liberties of equal citizenship, while the worth of liberty to persons and groups is proportional to their capacity to advance their ends within the framework the system defines' (TJ 179; see also JF 149, 150–1). Although Rawls uses the term 'capacity' in this explanation, it is fairly apparent that, in general, value is understood as being measured by those resources which an individual has at his or her disposal with which to make use of those liberties. Responding to this criticism, Rawls says that justice as fairness does indeed understand the Liberty Principle as guaranteeing *most* of the basic liberties merely formally, at least in the sense that it does not provide individuals with special resources to devote to using particular liberties. However, it is not the case that individuals living under justice as fairness considered as a whole would enjoy these liberties merely formally, of course: they would have the resources guaranteed to them by the second principle, and would be able to devote their resources to exercising their liberties as and when they judged best. So, according to Rawls, there are no grounds for subjecting justice as fairness as a whole to this criticism.

But only most of the liberties are guaranteed merely formally. One set of liberties is singled out for special treatment: the political liberties. These are guaranteed what Rawls calls 'fair value', which means, essentially, that political processes are to be insulated from the background inequalities permitted by the Difference Principle. This commitment would allow, for example, that private contributions to political campaigns and campaign expenditures be limited by law.

Conclusion

Rawls's theory is subject to two kinds of criticism. There are internal criticisms: claims that, given his fundamental premises, the principles do not follow. So, for example, even given the set-up of the Original Position, there is a case to be made that a less demanding principle than the Difference Principle would be adopted. Since the parties are bound to prioritize an 'acceptable outcome', why would they not settle for a principle that ensured a satisfactory outcome, rather than the best worst outcome, for all? Similarly it is not clear that the exact priority rules that Rawls specifies would be adopted within the Original Position: if each of the principles matters somewhat, could it really be the case that the prior principles *completely* outweigh the subordinate principles in *all* circumstances?

There are also external criticisms: claims that Rawls adopts the wrong framework, or that one or another of his principles is wrong, regardless of whether they are really implied by his framework. Most anglophone political philosophy since 1971 can be seen as consisting of either internal or external criticism of Rawls. In the next two chapters we shall focus on implied external criticisms: that Rawls chooses the wrong metric, in chapter 4; and that his principles are entirely wrong, in chapter 5. In chapter 6 we shall encounter both the external criticism that his theory is individualist in the wrong way, and the internal criticism that although the framework is entirely right, the logic of his theory supports a right to a cultural context of choice which, in turn, justifies group-differentiated rights which may, in some circumstances, conflict with and take precedence over individual rights.

4

The Capability Approach

I want to turn now to a perspective on justice which is increasingly influential on non-governmental organizations and the community of international policymakers. It is a variant of liberalism, which is not usually referred to as a theory, but as an approach – the capability approach. Rawls, remember, claims that what the state should be concerned about distributing are the social primary goods. We find out who the least advantaged are by looking at everybody's basket of social primary goods; those who have least are the least advantaged. But this is not the standard way that policymakers and economists have measured well-being. The standard measure of the relative wealth of different countries, for example, is gross domestic product, which is stated, simply, in terms of money. By contrast, economists tend to make interpersonal comparisons in terms of preference satisfaction: someone is considered better off than someone else if they have a higher level of preference satisfaction. The capability approach was developed by Amartya Sen as an alternative to these two ways of making interpersonal – and international – comparisons of well-being. But he also poses it as an alternative to Rawls's concentration on the social primary goods. In this chapter I shall outline the capability approach, as it is defended by Sen and as it had been developed by Martha Nussbaum, and look at the potential problems it faces (Nussbaum 2000; Sen 1999).

Before outlining the theory, though, it's worth noting that neither Sen nor Nussbaum offers the capability approach as a full theory of justice, in the way that Rawls claims completeness for his theory. The focus of the capability approach is just on what it is that the state should be concerned with distributing, not on the rule by which it should be distributed. Sen and Nussbaum both concentrate heavily on normative issues in international development policy, and they know full well that in the short to medium term capabilities are not going to be distributed equally or to the benefit of the least advantaged. So they argue that everyone should have at least a threshold level of basic capabilities. I am going to focus on the arguments for capabilities as the focus of justice, rather than on whether thresholds, equality or maximin should be the distributive rule.

Preference satisfaction, real income and primary goods

Why does Sen reject both preference satisfaction and real income as measures of well-being for the purposes of justice? Let's take preference satisfaction first. He objects to this for three reasons (Sen 1999: 62–3).

First, some preferences are what he calls *adaptive*. In other words, people have them not because there is any reason for them to believe that their fulfilment will meet their true interests, but because their circumstances have distorted their sense of what is in their true interests. So, for example, whether someone aspires to a professional career will depend, amongst other things, on whether the social structure will allow them to fulfil that aspiration. A woman may form the aspiration to become a wife and mother not because it would really serve her interests, but because it seems like the only realistic option. We cannot defend the policy of prohibiting her from having a professional career on the grounds that she has what she wants if the only reason that she wants what she wants is that we are prohibiting her from having a professional career.

Second, as we saw when discussing Rawls's defence of the social primary goods as the currency of justice, some preferences are expensive to fulfil, and others are not. The objection from adaptive preferences is motivated by worries that some people have preferences that it is too easy to meet, because they have dampened their aspirations excessively in response to injustice, and that some have preferences that are too expensive to meet, because they have failed to exercise a restraint on their aspirations. The normal person who has trained her tastes so that claret is needed to give her the same level of satisfaction as another person who is satisfied with a cup of tea should not be considered worse off from the point of view of justice just because she achieves less satisfaction than the person with less demanding tastes.

Finally, if one's focus is exclusively on preference satisfaction, or utility, one lacks the resources to account for the special value of rights, or liberties. A preference satisfaction standard cannot distinguish between the fundamental human interests that merit protection by rights, and those other interests that can sometimes legitimately be neglected for the sake of the fundamental interests of others (or of the person in question). This is especially problematic because the preference satisfaction metric does not distinguish between what we might call benign and offensive preferences. The only reason, on a preference satisfaction standard, for objecting to someone acting on a preference to do ill toward another is that it might conflict with the preferences of the other person. So as long as someone does not mind having their rights violated, or does not mind very much, the preference satisfaction standard does not object to it.[1]

These arguments against using preference satisfaction as a standard of people's well-being suggest that we look for objective measures of this criterion, which will not be susceptible to the objections. The most obvious is real income, or money. But, as Sen points out, using money as the measure of well-being has its own problems (Sen 1999: 70–2). People differ enormously in their ability to convert income into welfare. Some differences (having expensive tastes) they should take responsibility for. But others are beyond their control. So, for example, disabled people need resources additional to those that the ordinarily abled need in order to be able to do the same things. People who live in temperate climates need to spend less on heating and air-conditioning to achieve the same level of comfort as do people in extreme climates. The social climate varies: the personal insecurity of living in a society where crime is prevalent is a real loss of well-being which will not be captured by counting income. There are also differences in relational perspectives: being relatively poor in a rich society can lead to exclusion from public activities which can be enjoyed by people who are poorer in income terms, but relatively richer within their own societies. Finally, because income streams into family units, counting income tells us nothing about the distribution of income within the family. But households in which males consume most of the income may be much worse off than households in which the consumption is more equitably shared.

So much for preference satisfaction and real income as measures of well-being. Why isn't Sen satisfied with Rawls's measure – social primary goods? The social primary goods are, Sen says, subject to the same objections as income. They are objective goods, the measurement of which takes no account of the differences between people in their ability to convert them into well-being. The difference between the paraplegic and the ordinarily abled person does not show up when we simply look at their relative levels of social primary goods. The ordinarily abled person, in fact, looks worse off than the paraplegic if the paraplegic has the same bank balance and also a wheelchair. But that is ridiculous – on no measure should the paraplegic be considered better off.

Capabilities and functionings

Sen's alternative is to look at a relationship between the resources people have and what they can do with them. As he puts it, in a good theory of well-being, 'account would have to be taken not only of the primary goods the persons respectively hold, but also of the relevant personal characteristics that govern the conversion of primary goods into the person's ability to promote her ends' (Sen 1999: 74). What matters to people is that they are able to achieve actual *functionings*, that is, 'the actual living that people manage to achieve' (Sen 1999: 73). Walking is a functioning, so are eating, reading, mountain climbing and chatting. 'The concept of functionings . . . reflects the various things a person may value doing or being – varying from the basic (being adequately nourished) to the very complex (being able to take part in the life of the community)' (Sen 1999: 75). But when we make interpersonal comparisons of well-being we should find a measure which incorporates references to functionings, but also reflects the intuition that what matters is not merely achieving the functioning but being free to achieve it. So we should look at 'the freedom to achieve actual livings that one can have a reason to value' (Sen 1999: 73) or, to put it another way, 'substantive freedoms – the capabilities – to choose a life one has reason to value' (Sen 1999: 74). 'A person's capability refers to the alternative combinations of functionings that are feasible for her to achieve. Capability is thus a kind of freedom: the substantive freedom to achieve alternative functioning combinations' (Sen 1999: 75).

The notion of capability is essential for Sen, because someone's actual functionings need not tell us very much about how well off he or she is. Consider Tony, a stockbroker who suddenly abandons his job to fast in support of world peace, and Sid, a stockbroker who is suddenly marooned on a barren island. After a week their physical state might be identical: looking at their level of functioning will not tell us the difference. But there is a difference: Tony, unlike Sid, is capable of a high level of functioning. His low level of functioning is the result of a voluntary choice, unlike Sid's. The capabilities approach captures this difference by looking behind the actual functionings at the opportunities or freedom people have to function.

There are several problems with understanding the capability approach. The first, and most striking, is often called the indexing problem. There are an uncountable number of capabilities people might have, and not everyone can have all of them. How are we to compare people who have different sets of capabilities? To see how difficult this question is, think of Brian and Dougal. Brian is blind but otherwise is in good health and his other senses function well. Dougal is deaf, and has a painful, but not debilitating, chronic condition. Which of them is better off? In order to answer this we need to be able to compare the value of hearing with that of sight, and assess the significance of pain for overall functioning. It is not clear how to do this. And if that is difficult, it is nothing compared to the problem of comparing Brian and Dougal's situations with those of millions of other people who have some capabilities they lack, but lack others that they have.

A second problem concerns how perfectionist the theory is. The choice of capabilities rather than functionings reflects Sen's concern with personal choice and freedom. Nevertheless, if we examine the definition of capabilities, he does not call them opportunities or freedoms to do whatever we want to do, or value doing. He counts only those functionings people 'have reason to value' or 'have reason to want to achieve'. This suggests, what is certainly true, that some functionings are ones that people do not have reasons to value or want to achieve. On the capability approach someone who achieves functionings they have no reason to value is worse off than someone who achieves what are intuitively fewer functionings which they nevertheless have reason to value. But Sen pretty much leaves it at that. Moral philosophers commonly make a distinction between internal and external reasons. External reasons are reasons that are compelling regardless of whether or not the agent recognizes them (I have a reason to eat healthily, even if I do not recognize that eating healthily is good); whereas internal reasons are those which the agent him- or herself 'has'. If Sen has internal reasons in mind, then the view is not very perfectionist, but it is redundant for him to mention them in the definition of capabilities. If he has external reasons in mind, the view might be quite perfectionist. The evangelical Christian believes that we all have (external) reasons to obey God's will, and we all have no (external) reasons to reject God's will, so the evangelical Christian could accept Sen's definition of capabilities, but have very little regard for personal freedom, since the only capabilities which would count would be capabilities to execute God's will.

I think this in itself is a good reason to suppose that Sen's theory is not intended to be excessively perfectionistic. On most views of the good consistent with a liberal approach any individual might be capable of a wide range of goods, and can only (in practice) realize a few of them. So it is very difficult to be an attentive and involved parent while simultaneously being a world-beating mountain climber – and for many people at least, it might be possible to achieve either, but not both, of those goods. People can have (external) reasons for valuing diverse and conflicting goods. And it is entirely possible for them to have reasons to value things which are not (in fact) good; just as it is possible for us to have reasons to believe things which are not, in fact, true. Given this, the focus on capabilities is what renders the theory liberal: it focuses on freedom and opportunity rather than achievement.

The indexing problem

Martha Nussbaum's development of the theory is more sensitive than Sen's to concerns about perfectionism, and is more directly interested in addressing the indexing problem. Nussbaum explains that the capability approach aims to provide a theory that is political in Rawls's sense – that is, one that can be endorsed from within a wide range of more restricted conceptions of what gives human life value. She elaborates a list of ten basic capabilities, which, she thinks, everyone could accept as essential contributions to human flourishing. These ten capabilities between them constitute a threshold below which it is particularly unjust for a society to let any individual fall. So even though justice may have something – even a great deal – to say about inequalities above this threshold, ensuring that everyone meets this threshold is the most urgent matter for all societies in which any individual falls below it. Her list follows (Nussbaum 2000: 78–80):

1 *Life*: being able to live to the end of a human life of normal length.
2 *Bodily health*: being able to have good health, nourishment and shelter.
3 *Bodily integrity*: being able to move freely about, to have opportunities for sexual satisfaction, reproductive choices, and being able to be secure against physical violations.

4   *Senses, imagination, and thought*: being able to imagine, think and reason in a 'truly human' way, and having the education necessary to exercise these capabilities.

5   *Emotions*: 'in general, [being able] to love, to grieve, to experience longing, gratitude and justified anger' (Nussbaum 2000: 79).

6   *Practical reason*: being able to form a conception of the good and engage in critical reflection about the planning of one's life.

7   *Affiliation*:
(a)   being able to live with and toward others, to recognize and show concern for other human beings.
(b)   having the social bases of self-respect and non-humiliation; being able to be treated as a dignified being with equal worth.

8   *Other species*: being able to live with concern for and in relation to animals, plants and the world of nature.

9   *Play*: being able to laugh, play and recreate.

10   *Control over environment*:
(a)   *Political*: being able to participate effectively in political choices that govern one's life.
(b)   *Material*: having real opportunities to hold property, seek employment on an equal basis with others, having freedom from unwarranted search and seizure.

Nussbaum doesn't make much of an argument for the list, or for the idea that the list would be able to command an 'overlapping consensus', but that should not be held against her. Her basic idea is that certain capabilities 'exert a moral claim that they should be developed' (Nussbaum 2000: 83), and hence act as the grounds for political claims on government. The fact that they exert a moral claim is itself evidence that they could command a consensus, and while it is possible to imagine someone flourishing without using some of Nussbaum's capabilities, it is hard to imagine them realistically thinking that everyone else could flourish without having the capabilities. They do, indeed, seem to have the centrality she claims for them.

The list doesn't *exactly* solve the indexing problem that Sen's version of the theory faces. But by singling out as particularly important a set of capabilities that make substantial demands on resources, it *partially* solves the problem. We can say of anyone who does not have all the ten basic capabilities that they are worse off than someone who has all ten. Furthermore, although, as we shall see, the capabilities cannot be traded off against one another, two are particularly important, because they infuse the other capabilities. Without Practical Reason and Affiliation, people cannot flourish as they exercise the other capabilities, so it is fair to say that someone who lacks these two capabilities is worse off than another who has them, but lacks others. Nussbaum also distinguishes three categories of capability:

1   *Basic capabilities*: These are the innate equipment of individuals, without which it is impossible to develop and exercise the more advanced capabilities (Nussbaum 2000: 84).
2   *Internal capabilities*: These are developed states that are sufficient conditions for the exercise of requisite functions. These, unlike the innate equipment, are internal states of the person which develop (usually) in response to the environment in which the person is raised. So sexual functioning is an internal capability; it requires a certain level of physical maturity, but also that one not have been psychologically or physically damaged by one's environment. Most people, Nussbaum says, have the internal capability for religious freedom and freedom of speech (Nussbaum 2000: 84). But, of course, whether they can actually exercise their freedom of speech, or sexual choices, depends on their current environment – on whether the external conditions allow them to do so.
3   *Combined capabilities*: These are internal capabilities combined with suitable external conditions for the exercise of the function (Nussbaum 2000: 84–5). The combined capability for freedom of speech is present when someone has the relevant internal capability and lives in an environment which supports its use.

The relationship between these different kinds of capability helps guide policy: it is vital to provide the conditions both for the development of the internal capabilities and for their exercise. The indexing problem is solved sufficiently well to give us a good deal of guidance when formulating public policy and when evaluating the relative well-being of different countries.

I said that the separate components on the list are not supposed to be interchangeable. Nussbaum thinks that having more of one does not compensate for having less of another below the threshold (though it may be perfectly sensible for people to trade them off against each other above the relevant threshold). Nussbaum, consistently with Sen, includes on the list some of what Rawls calls 'natural goods'. Health, for example, is a natural good – it is not something that society can take and distribute (as it can, for example, money). But differences in health states are often socially caused, and governments can do a great deal to affect who has good and bad health both by distributing healthcare, and by distributing the goods (education, nutrition, freedom from pollutants) which influence whether someone has good or bad health.[2] Nussbaum observes the intuition that when nature causes some inequality of capability, justice has less to say about the inequality than when government action (or inaction) is the cause. But because nature is, in fact, highly responsive to government action, governments are often culpable of (and justice often impugns) a maldistribution of natural goods, like health.

Like Sen, Nussbaum is deeply concerned with respecting the practical reasoning of moral agents. They must have the space, or freedom, to make and act on their own judgements about how to live their lives, and how to act toward others, at least within some very wide limits. Thus she agrees with Sen that capabilities rather than functionings are the proper measure of well-being. But, again like Sen, her approach is mildly perfectionistic but in a way that she takes the trouble to explain. Nussbaum is openly willing to license the state to force functionings upon people (or, more normally, to forcibly prevent them from doing things which jeopardize their continued capabilities). The grounds are that the more central a capability is to overall functioning, the more reluctant we should be to allow people, even voluntarily, to give it up. This is a familiar position with respect to children: we think that the state is entitled to force children to attend school even if they would rather not, in order to foster the development of their capabilities, and that parents are entitled to force their children to eat nutritious food, and to prohibit them from sticking their fingers into electrical outlets, for their own long-term benefit. Nussbaum applies different standards to adults, but the principle is the same: paternalism toward adults is justified in a number of areas, where *we force functionings to protect capabilities*. So, for example, it is reasonable on her view to prohibit – or at least highly to regulate – suicide, since life is a prerequisite of any functioning. Similarly, selling oneself into slavery forecloses on future opportunities for functioning, in a way that joining a religious sect, for example, doesn't. But health and safety regulations are also justified, because information is hard for individuals to secure, making informed choice extremely difficult. Laws requiring automobile users to wear seat-belts and motorcyclists to wear helmets are justified because we do not want individuals to bear the cost of momentary carelessness; and some pharmaceuticals may be regulated because of the long-term and irreversible impairment of capabilities to which they can give rise. Nussbaum goes so far as to argue that even voluntary female genital mutilation might properly be prohibited, on the grounds that it involves a permanent removal of the capacity for sexual pleasure: 'It seems plausible for governments to ban female genital mutilation, even when practiced without coercion: for, in addition to long-term health risks, the practice involves the permanent removal of the capability for most sexual pleasure, although individuals should of course be free to choose not to have sexual pleasure if they prefer not to' (Nussbaum 2000: 94).

This last prohibition may seem surprising. Of course, most genital mutilation is done to children, without their consent (or without consent that counts, since it comes from children), so it is not voluntary. But Nussbaum is claiming that even when adults voluntarily want to impose it on themselves they may be prohibited. The person who wants to refrain from having sexual pleasure, she says, can do that, regardless of whether they have mutilated genitalia, and the cost of foreclosing on one possibly vital future source of flourishing is so drastic that we might be justified in preventing people from doing it. Nussbaum ties this possible prohibition to the value of bodily integrity, but that is slightly misleading. There are lots of things we do (or don't do) to our bodies which influence considerably our long-term functionings just as drastically, but which could not be prohibited (or forced) on those grounds. By refraining from ever practising yoga I have, presumably, foreclosed on certain future activities. Certainly by refraining from practising tennis or swimming I have done this, and at 40 I think it is reasonable for me to think that I shall never enjoy those things, so that if some invasion of my bodily integrity enhanced my ability to do something else that I do value at the cost that I could never do those things, it would be hard to justify prohibiting me. What if someone experiences their sexual desires as deeply unwelcome interferences in their ability to live a calm and contented life? They just want to 'get on' with life, and not have to deal with the desires which assault them. Why should they not be permitted to excise a source of desire which they experience not as an avenue for flourishing, but as a barrier to pursuing their chosen ends?

An answer is available to Nussbaum which doesn't appeal to bodily integrity, but appeals instead to the demands of practical reason. Irreversible excision of the source of this person's desires is problematic because it forecloses permanently on one, important, possible revision of her desires or conception of how to live her life. In seeking the treatment, she is treating her current set of commitments as unrevisable, as permanent in an implausible way. But, furthermore, it is an assault on the capability for practical reason. One is no longer faced with the challenge of controlling and responding to one's desires. Part of the value of practical reason is that it allows a person to be an author of her life on a day-to-day basis, rather than following a script which, even if she wrote it, was written in advance. Reflecting on and negotiating one's own desires, however inconvenient one experiences them as being, is part of what it is to be fully human.[3]

In making these comments, I am not meaning to endorse Nussbaum's position on female genital mutilation, and in fact she holds that position very tentatively. Instead I am trying to illuminate the plausibility of the more general idea she relies on, that despite the value of personal freedom, there may be some self-regarding activities that the state can legitimately forbid (or try to prevent), when those activities would substantially diminish the person's capacity for living a fully human life.

Notice, too, that Nussbaum's approach gives guidance in the case of paternalistic action regarding children and their upbringings, especially to policymakers. Children are generally taken to be appropriate objects of paternalistic action because they do not yet fully enjoy the developed capabilities that make paternalism inappropriate. They are targets of paternalistic action from several sources, and two, in particular, concern us: their parents and the state. Their parents usually have considerable licence to make judgements about what will be good for them, but it is more difficult for the state to assess their good either as the children that they are or as the adults they will become. Nussbaum's list suggests that the state is responsible for ensuring that children have the resources and education necessary for them to come to enjoy an adequate range of basic capabilities in adulthood, and the state's regulation of children's education should reflect this. Of course, this will involve the state in forcing certain functionings in order to ensure future capabilities for those functionings. Most of us do not learn truly foreign languages without being forced to in school; nor do we learn complex mathematics, or how to appreciate Shakespeare, without a degree of coercion. What the capability approach recognizes is that refraining from forcing children to do some things is tantamount to denying them the opportunities to do those things later in life.

Nussbaum argues that the capability approach gives us a natural way of understanding talk about human rights. Sometimes when politicians talk about rights they talk as if rights are basic: the starting point of discussion. But this is an artifice of the constraints on political debate. Constitutions guarantee rights, and they have *de facto* political authority, so people appeal to them. But constitutions can be wrong: they can guarantee rights that, in fact, nobody should have, and can fail to guarantee rights everyone should have. In order to get clear about what rights people should have – in order to be able to evaluate the constitutions themselves – we need a prior moral criterion. This is what the capability approach provides. By specifying basic interests that everyone has in common, and by showing that some adequate protection of those interests is essential for enabling people to live fully human lives, the capability approach provides a moral under-pinning for rights claims. On Nussbaum's list it is clear why people should have a right to education, to freedom of religion, to vote, and not at all clear why they should have a right to bear arms. Nussbaum describes some rights as combined capabilities, because they involve having both the external conditions and the internal capabilities that enable one to do something (the rights to political participation, free religious exercise, etc.). But I think it is more illuminating to think of capabilities as the bases of rights claims. If someone claims that there is a fundamental right to X, it is incumbent on them to justify it; and justification will proceed by showing how the right to X is required to serve some capability. If there is no capability which it serves, then it is not a fundamental right.

Justice as fairness and the capability approach

I want to finish this chapter by comparing the capability approach with Rawls's theory of justice, on two dimensions. The first is that Nussbaum, at least, shares Rawls's aspiration for a theory that is 'political' in the sense that it can win allegiance from within a wide range of conceptions of the good life. She says she seeks a theory that is 'political, rather than comprehensive, in the sense that it urges us to respect the many different conceptions of the good citizens may have, and to foster a political climate in which they will be able to pursue the good according to their own lights, so long as they do no harm to others' (Nussbaum 2000: 59). The list of basic capabilities is supposed to be political in this sense because its items are all recognized as goods by a wide range of conceptions of the good. Theories that are political in this sense walk a fine line. On the one hand the moral ideas underlying the theory must have enough content to be able to generate a theory of justice that makes real demands on social institutions. So, for example, it has to be able to generate principles that tell us what rules should guide the distribution of resources, and should be able to tell us what stance to take toward the basic liberties, and something about what their content should be. A theory that appealed to no moral ideas at all would, presumably, be unable to do this. On the other hand the theory has to appeal to sufficiently few and modest moral ideas that it is not in deep conflict with a wide range of really existing conceptions of the good life.

No theory of justice can command the allegiance of adherents of *all* existing conceptions of the good: how could a fundamentalist Muslim, a Hollywood liberal, a Southern Baptist, and a Trotskyist all agree on a single, determinate, theory of justice, without at least some of them abandoning their initial views? But neither Nussbaum nor Rawls has this ambition. Rawls limits himself to seeking support from within reasonable conceptions of the good, which he defines as doctrines which 'recognize the burdens of judgment and so, among other political values, that of liberty of conscience' (JF 191). Neither Nussbaum nor Rawls suggests that adherents of even reasonable conceptions of the good will immediately recognize the truth of their respective theories of justice. Instead they think that the theories, by appealing to widely shareable values, can, over time, come to command support as people come to recognize the value of living in accordance with them, and come to adjust their conceptions of the good to accommodate these values.

Is the search for a political theory of justice oppressive? Some might argue that it is. A political theory of justice disregards the views of those who are unable to recognize the burdens of judgement, for whatever reason, and accords their allegiance less weight than those whose substantive doctrines do recognize such burdens. As Rawls himself points out, the educational regime his theory recommends may lead people to abandon unreasonable doctrines because it will encourage them to think of themselves as members of a secular state with all the rights and liberties that go along with that, rather than as being bound to the laws and norms of the religious community in which they are raised (JF 156). But it is important to note that this is not part of the justification or aim of politically liberal justice. Political liberalism, whether of Rawls's or Nussbaum's kind, is justified by its aim of distributing the fruits of social cooperation fairly, and both kinds of liberalism involve strong guarantees of freedom of conscience, religion and association. Traditionalists can complain that their view will find it hard to survive in a liberal order, but they cannot complain that the liberal order is designed to make it difficult, nor can they elaborate an alternative which does not impose the same burden on those who hold different, but reasonable, views.

The second comparison takes us back to Sen's criticism of the primary goods metric. How different are the capability and primary goods approaches really? Both Sen and Nussbaum compare capabilities favourably with primary goods. But Rawls does not only disagree with that favourable comparison; he denies that it is the relevant comparison to make. Instead, he says:

> The account of primary goods does take into account, and does not abstract from, basic capabilities: namely, the capabilities of citizens as free and equal persons in virtue of their two moral powers. It is these powers that enable them to be normal and fully cooperating members of society over a complete life and to maintain their status as free and equal citizens. We rely on a conception of citizens' capabilities and basic needs, and the equal rights and liberties are specified with these moral powers in mind. (JF 169)

In other words, the social primary goods are justified in terms of their service of the basic capability, and are supposed to help heuristically with the indexing problem that, as we have seen, afflicts the capability approach. What is different between the social primary goods and Sen's version of the capability approach, at least, is that the primary goods constitute a publicly measurable metric. This has three advantages. First, citizens can see more readily whether justice is being done if we have a public way of measuring it. Second, the theory can guide policymaking more clearly, because policymakers can see what the relevant deficits are. Finally, and deriving from the other two advantages, citizens can more easily hold policymakers accountable for their successes and failures, by looking at the publicly measurable outcomes of the policies.

However close justice as fairness and the capability approach are in theory, one thing is clear. Both theories require extensive redistribution of income and wealth away from existing distributions, both within rich countries, and between rich and poor countries. In addition, both theories would require extensive redistribution away from the distributive outcomes of free markets. I want to turn, then, to a variety of theories that object to such redistribution.

5
Libertarian Justice

One criticism of liberal egalitarian justice that I have so far neglected is the objection that redistribution of income and wealth required by egalitarian theories is unacceptable because it constitutes an unjust violation of the property rights of those who are taxed. This chapter will take up this objection, by discussing two different versions of libertarian justice: the general theory that justice involves extensive rights to private property, such that only very minimal taxation is ever legitimate, and that it is hardly ever legitimate when its grounds are unrelated to the good of those who are being taxed.

The two versions of libertarianism that I shall discuss have both been extremely influential in public life in the English-speaking world, and beyond – probably more influential than any other theory discussed in the book, with the possible exception of the capability approach discussed in the previous chapter. Before introducing particular defences of libertarian justice, it is important to say a word about property rights. People sometimes talk as if property rights over some object are simple: either you own something, in which case you can do what you want with it, or you do not own it, in which case you cannot. But in fact when somebody owns something in law they usually have a bundle of rights over it, and those rights vary from context to context. Typically, ownership of a house, even when the title is not mortgaged, includes the right to inhabit the house, but not the right to keep crocodiles in it; or even the right to store garbage indefinitely in the basement. In many jurisdictions, zoning laws limit the right to derive income from one's property. One may require permission to put a building to commercial use, and different permissions for different kinds of commercial use.

Libertarians typically do not claim that the right to property is absolute in the sense that people should be allowed to do absolutely anything with their property; and they also typically allow that one's income can be taxed for the purpose of maintaining what they call the minimal state – a state devoted to maintaining effective national defence, upholding the rule of law, and protecting private property. What they do typically argue, and what distinguishes libertarian from egalitarian approaches, is that justice supports a particularly strong set of property rights, such that taxation for redistributive purposes cannot be just.

A second preliminary is to note a couple of formal differences between liberal egalitarianism and libertarianism. Liberal egalitarianism is typically understood as a cluster of principles which bear considerable similarity – equality with respect to resources and/or opportunities being one of the central principles. Egalitarian liberals agree about the basic principles of justice; or, at least, their disagreements fall within a very restricted range. But they may disagree a great deal about what the world would look like if those principles were implemented: for example, Rawlsians differ enormously in *how much* inequality they think that the difference principle will justify in the real world. But libertarians typically do not share a theory of justice (or the broad brushstrokes of one); in fact some libertarians (like the Austrian economist Friedrich Hayek) disavow the idea of justice altogether (Hayek 1960). What unites libertarians is a constitutional prescription – we need a state, and it should place great priority on protecting private property in productive resources, with an emphasis on the efficacy of real market mechanisms. The state is there just to keep the market working, to protect our personal liberty, and to solve certain public goods problems (those which can be expected to produce more inefficiencies than the involvement of the state will produce itself). Twentieth-century libertarianism arose as a reaction against

Marxism, and especially Marxism's more complex offspring, social democracy. Liberal egalitarianism, which, unlike either of those two movements, has very little public currency, arose as an intellectual reaction to the inadequacies of utilitarianism, Marxist political theory and libertarianism itself.

Friedman on freedom

Milton Friedman calls himself a classical liberal, rather than a libertarian. He views the state as having a wide range of legitimate functions, including facilitating the production of public goods and restricting the production of public bads. But his work has been extremely influential on politicians and economists who are opposed to taxation specifically for redistributive purposes – it has been, perhaps, the most politically influential theory since the mid-point of the twentieth century. So I shall start this chapter by looking at Friedman's theory, and go on to look at the more definitively libertarian theory of Robert Nozick.

Friedman grounds what he calls 'classical' or 'economic' liberalism in the value of freedom, which value supports very strong property rights. Friedman is primarily an economist, not a philosopher, so it may seem odd to treat him in a book of this kind, but in fact his theory has a clear moral foundation, and is institutionally more nuanced than some libertarian (and, for that matter, non-libertarian) alternatives.

Friedman's central argument for libertarianism is that there is a deep connection between economic freedom – a system which accords extremely strong protections to individual rights to own and use property – and political freedom – a political system in which individuals are broadly free to pursue their lives according to their own lights, with minimal interference by the government. This connection is not *identity*: if the two systems were identical, then all we would need do would be to implement political freedom and we would, in doing so, be implementing economic freedom (and vice versa). The connection, instead, is the following: political and individual freedom can only be achieved in systems of economic freedom.

Economic freedom is 'itself a component of freedom broadly understood, so economic freedom is also an end in itself. In the second place economic freedom is also an indispensable means toward the achievement of political freedom' (Friedman 1962: 8). Friedman defines individual, or personal, freedom, as 'the absence of coercion of a man by his fellow men' (Friedman 1962: 15). The crucial point here is that freedom is being unconstrained by other persons acting as individuals or collectively through some agency (like the state); freedom is inhibited only by the acts of other persons.

I should deflect, straightaway, a couple of rather obvious objections to the idea that freedom in this sense is a value that should guide the design of social institutions. The first is that freedom should not be a fundamental value, because what matters is human flourishing, and people's own judgements about how to act are only at best poor guides as to what will enable them to flourish. Sometimes people's preferences are ill informed, or bad for them. So freedom is an instrumental good only – it matters only in so far as and because it promotes human flourishing. The second objection is that Friedman's conception of freedom is not what we normally mean by freedom. On our more normal understanding, someone is free to do something if there is no external force preventing her, and her freedom is compromised even if the force preventing her is not human. So someone who gets trapped in a cave because of an avalanche of rocks is not free to leave, even though there is no human coercion involved.

Friedman's response to the first objection allows us to construct a response to the second. Friedman says that freedom is crucially important because it enables us to live an ethical life. To live an ethical life one needs freedom, because one needs to develop and exercise the capability to modify one's preferences in response to negotiated experience:

> A major aim of the liberal is to leave the ethical problem for the individual to wrestle with. The 'really' important ethical problems are those that face an individual in a free society – what he should do with his freedom. There are thus two sets of values that a liberal will emphasize – the values that are relevant to relations among people, which is the context in which he assigns priority to freedom; and the values that are

relevant to the individual in the exercise of his freedom, which is the realm of individual ethics and philosophy. (Friedman 1962: 12)

This response emphasizes human agency, and as such it provides the means to respond to the second objection. The reason why humanly imposed constraints matter so much is that they are a direct reflection of human agency: there is something that other moral agents can clearly do about them. This makes them a matter of justice, or, to put it differently, a matter of concern from the perspective of the state, in a way that the non-humanly imposed constraints are not.

It is individual freedom that serves our interest in being able to make and execute our own judgements, to live our lives according to the ethical principles we have been left to wrestle with. Coercion does not have to be intentional in order to be coercive: Friedman says that what is wrong with certain 'neighbourhood effects' is that they are instances of coercion, even though, by definition, they involve no intention to coerce. For example, when a factory-owner pollutes a river which he does not have property rights in, he thereby coerces those who live downstream, and who are forced to choose between finding alternative sources of water or cleaning the previously clean water.

Economic freedom is a component of personal freedom. In so far as one's economic transactions with others are uncoerced, one is free (in Friedman's sense) with respect to those transactions. Friedman understands economic freedom as freedom of contract: it is encroached upon by any government restrictions on the validity of contracts except when justified by bona fide concerns about externalities. So, for Friedman, capitalism is the only economic system which can realize economic freedom institutionally. But of course there are many different ways of running a capitalist economy, and Friedman's theory implies that economic freedom is most fully realized when the state refrains, for the most part, from redistributing income and wealth away from the distributions realized in the market, and when it interferes with the working of the market only in order to regulate the money supply, prevent the emergence of monopolies, and protect property rights (through copyright and patenting law, for example). The best system is what he calls a 'free private enterprise exchange economy . . . competitive capitalism' (Friedman 1962: 13).

Non-competitive practices, and market failures in general, are problematic for Friedman, not only because they are inefficient, but also because they make coercion more likely, and thus promote violations of freedom. Consider the clearest kinds of market failure: negative externalities. Suppose that the owner of a factory upstream starts to pollute the stream, and the farmer downstream now has a choice between drinking the polluted water or cleaning it. The farmer has had a cost imposed on her, and her set of available options has been restricted, by the conscious actions of the polluter. That is just coercion, for Friedman. He is careful not to say that the government should always intervene in market failures, partly because he doubts the wisdom of governments, partly because he doubts their motives, and partly because he recognizes that government action has its costs too. But he is clear that in principle market failures legitimate government intervention.

Friedman makes two very different kinds of argument for the connection between capitalism and freedom. First he makes an optimistic induction that economic freedom is *a prerequisite for* political freedom (a central component of, and in this argument a proxy for, individual freedom), because political freedom has only been widespread in capitalist regimes. 'Political freedom in this instance clearly came along with the free market and the development of capitalist institutions. So also did political freedom in the golden age of Greece and in the early days of the Roman era. History suggests only that capitalism is a necessary condition for political freedom' (Friedman 1962: 9–10). He acknowledges that capitalism does not *guarantee* political freedom: Germany from 1932 to 1941 was recognizably capitalist, as is contemporary Singapore, and there are plenty of other examples. But, he thinks, no non-capitalist society has achieved political freedom, whereas many capitalist societies have achieved a reasonable degree of political freedom (Friedman 1962: 10–11).

The second argument is more general (Friedman 1962: 15–26, examples 16–20). Friedman argues as follows:

'Political freedom means the absence of coercion of a man by his fellow men. The fundamental threat to freedom is the power to coerce, the preservation of freedom requires the elimination of . . . concentration of power to the fullest possible extent and the dispersal and distribution of whatever power cannot be eliminated' (Friedman 1962: 15). But if economic power is concentrated in the loci of political power (the state and its local agencies, such as regional and city governments), then economic power cannot act as a check on political power. If, by contrast, economic power is distanced from the loci of political power – for example, by maximizing the holdings of economic resources in private hands – then it can, practically, act as a check on political power. But the best – if not the only – way of keeping political power separate from political power is by allowing a free market. Widespread private ownership of productive resources, regulated as little as is needed to keep the market functioning effectively, is the best way of maintaining political freedom.

Friedman gives a particular example. Under capitalism, advocacy of radical change (one of the elements of political freedom) can be secured by the profit-seeking behaviour of private owners. They will seek to produce the literature which makes them a profit – and they will therefore produce left-wing magazines when they can make money that way, which they will be able to if there is a significant market for left-wing ideas. But there is probably no way for a socialist government which owns the printing presses to do this – certainly, there is no way to *secure* the freedom to advocate radical change. Because the government itself is the institution distributing the means to criticize the government, it has no incentive to make those resources available. Of course, left-wing propaganda threatens the capitalist system, so the capitalist class in general also has a reason to oppose making paper and newsprint available to left-wing critics of capitalism. But each individual capitalist firm faces only a fraction of the threat posed by left-wing propaganda, whereas each firm that sells the newsprint and paper gains enormously from the sale of the goods. So the capitalist class has a serious collective action problem which, in Friedman's capitalism, it cannot overcome. Capitalism therefore facilitates criticism of capitalism better than any other system facilitates criticism of itself.

Neither of Friedman's arguments is very successful, at least in supporting the kind of property rights regime that libertarians favour. Consider the first argument. It is true that only more or less capitalist economies have enjoyed constitutional rule and widespread freedom in Friedman's sense. But so-called 'socialist' regimes have typically come to be in extremely unfavourable circumstances, and the sample of regimes that have enjoyed widespread freedoms overall is very small, far too small for us to be confident in any sort of induction.

More importantly, capitalist economies vary enormously in the amount of redistribution of income their governments engage in, and there is no reason to think that the security of robust property rights enhances the amount of freedom (even in Friedman's sense) relative to, for example, egalitarian social-democratic regimes. So, for example, there is no reason to believe that in Sweden and the Netherlands, where the government engages in a great deal of redistribution from rich to poor, there is less freedom than in Britain or the United States, where there is much less redistribution away from market outcomes, and people are much more unequally situated.

Friedman does not offer any way of measuring freedom across large populations, so the claim that egalitarian social democracies are no more unfree than free market capitalisms is hard to establish, though for the same reason it is hard to refute. But what Friedman does tell us about freedom, crucially, implies that freedom is denied when property rights are upheld as well as when redistribution is practised. The conception of liberty is 'absence of effective coercion from one's fellow man'. Now, think of the following case: Julian owns an acre of property. Sandy, Charles and Fiona want to walk on it. Julian wants to look at it without a single person on it, feeling like the lord of all he surveys. If Julian is granted secure exclusive use rights to the land, as he wants, then the land has to be secured against Sandy, Charles and Fiona. Coercive sanctions must be imposed to prevent anyone other than Julian from using it. Typically, in a capitalist society governed by the rule of law these sanctions will be imposed by law, and enforced by the coercive machinery of the state. Julian's freedom with respect to the piece of property is

Charles's, Fiona's and Sandy's unfreedom with respect to it.

It is a special feature of freedom with respect to property that it is, if you like, competitive in this way. The right to freedom of expression, for example, is not – everyone can speak at once, and although that is not a particularly fruitful arrangement, it is one in which all, simultaneously, enjoy the same freedom. Infringements of the right to freedom of expression typically target some people rather than others, but when those restrictions are lifted, the people whose freedom was never restricted are not thereby made less free with respect to their expression. But when Charles's and Fiona's freedom with respect to Julian's property is increased, his is decreased.

Friedman might respond to this criticism by saying that the property is Julian's, so Charles, Fiona and Sandy have no right to be free with respect to it. That may be so – but the issue here is whose property it is. If Friedman is going to justify rights to private property and, in particular, against redistribution away from market outcomes by appeal to the value of freedom, he has no right to justify Charles and Fiona's unfreedom by appeal to the claim that Julian owns the property. There's simply no reason to believe that strong property rights promote freedom.

The Julian example raises another problem that Friedman never actually addresses. In the example, freedom with respect to some particular piece of property is unequally distributed, and freedom is directly competitive, so that protecting one person's freedom involves us in denying someone else's. Friedman's enthusiasm for capitalism is grounded in the idea that it promotes freedom. But whose freedom? He gives no account of how freedom may permissibly be distributed. But if freedom, in some of its aspects, is competitive, then when we promote freedom we must be sensitive to how it is distributed. In the case of property this boils down to the question of how property is distributed: the more equally it is distributed, the more equally freedom to use property is distributed. If freedom matters for the reasons Friedman thinks, and if everybody counts, then it would be wrong to choose a system in which we maximized freedom, but in which some people had little or no freedom. In fact if everyone counts as much as everyone else, then we should want equal freedom, or at least that everyone should have a reasonable opportunity to live an ethical life. If owning property is so central to being free, then, in principle, considerable redistribution away from market outcomes is permitted.

Notice this objection accepts a central premise of Friedman's – that freedom as he understands it matters a great deal. It also accepts his critique of collective ownership, and argues for more equal individual ownership (or at least is compatible with that). His argument has a hint of plausibility when directed against collectivist projects (like Soviet Communism) but much less when directed against redistributive projects (like European social democracy).

Now consider Friedman's second argument, from the incompatibility of political freedom with the centralization of economic power. There are several things to notice about this argument. The first is that Friedman is rather optimistic about the inability of capitalists to solve their collective action problem concerning dissenting speech. Some Marxists have talked as if capitalists all have all their interests in common, and that is obviously not true: the capitalist world's centres of power are full of lobbyists for corporations competing with each other for state subsidies, different environmental regulations, contrary trade practices, and so on. But in many circumstances very few corporations stand to gain from a flourishing anti-capitalist press, even if that press is very popular, and other corporations, if they feel threatened, may find it relatively easy to press for severe censorship, and certainly face a less serious collective action problem than do the multitude of relatively poor working-class people who might be attracted to such a press. Friedman's arguments may seem compelling at a time when there is hardly any demand for a robust anti-capitalist press, and when free market capitalism seems entrenched in most developed societies, but capitalist corporations have either actively supported or refrained from resisting restrictions on the freedom to dissent at times when dissent has been more widespread and threatening than it is now.

Again, it is worth mentioning that even conceding Friedman's general point that the freedom to dissent is going to be insecure if economic power is concentrated in the hands of the state, this does nothing to support the strong rights against redistribution that he argues for. In fact, redistributing wealth, if it can be done efficiently, is a way of diffusing economic power. Friedman has given us a reason for rejecting widespread nationalization of the means of production, but not a reason for resisting a more equal ownership of the means of production. But before leaving Friedman I want to comment that this objection to socialism was, in fact, anticipated by an early statist thinker, Lenin. In the period immediately preceding the Russian Revolution, Lenin worried about how competitive political debate could be guaranteed after the state had seized control of the mechanisms for public debate, and offered this solution:

> State power in the shape of the Soviets takes all the printing presses and all the newsprint and distributes them equitably; the state should come first ... the big parties should come second – say those that have polled one or two hundred thousand votes in both capitals. The smaller parties should come third and then any group of citizens which has a certain number of members or has collected a certain number of signatures. (Lenin 1964: 283)

Lenin's particular solution is unappealing for a number of reasons, and once in power the Bolsheviks were considerably less troubled by such niceties as this. The point of mentioning it is to show that the state can distribute resources for public debate equitably, and in a way that guarantees fair resources to dissidents, without resorting to private ownership and the price mechanism.

Nozick on entitlement

Unlike Friedman, Robert Nozick has Rawls's theory of justice in mind, and his book *Anarchy, State and Utopia* (1974) is conceived as a counterblast to it. Nozick's position is motivated not directly by a concern with freedom, but by an underlying concern with what he calls (following Rawls) the 'separateness of persons'. The 'separateness of persons' expresses the idea that individual persons each matter from the moral point of view, and that benefits to 'society' cannot justify violations of the persons of individuals. The common good, for Nozick, is made up of the good of individual persons, and has no independent standing. So whereas individual persons might make sacrifices of some of their interests for the sake of benefits to other of their interests (they diet for the sake of their health), society can never be justified in sacrificing the interests of some individuals for the sake of others. There is, Nozick says, 'no *social entity* with a good that undergoes some sacrifice for its own good. There are only individual people, different individual people, with their own individual lives. Using one of these people for the benefit of others, uses him and benefits the others. Nothing more' (Nozick 1974: 32–3).

Nozick thinks that the 'separateness of persons' thesis supports the existence of certain moral side-constraints on action toward people. These describe things that we may never do to other people (and that the state may never do to them on our behalf, or its own), because doing those things would amount to treating them as mere means to our own interests or well-being. So, it is commonly believed that it would be wrong of a jury to convict a suspect of a crime if they knew that he was innocent, even if they believed that in convicting him they would be sparing society some great social bad – for example, riots consequent on what the majority believed was a wrongful acquittal. The idea of a moral side-constraint is supposed to manifest an absolute prohibition of this kind. Think of it this way: there are certain kinds of cost we must never impose on someone, even if, from a personal cost–benefit analysis, these seem justified by the benefits for others that they would bring about.

I shall not question Nozick's claim that there are such side-constraints, although it is by no means an uncontroversial claim, as we shall see in the next chapter. But, accepting that there are such side-constraints, the interesting question is going to be: just what are they? As Nozick says, 'political philosophy is concerned only with certain ways that persons must not use others: primarily, physically aggressing against them' (Nozick 1974: 32), which he takes to be the most natural reading of the prescription by the eighteenth-century philosopher Immanuel Kant that we should 'act in such a way that you always treat humanity, whether in your own person or in the person of any other, never simply as a means, but always at the same time as an end' (Kant 1998: 38). But given the permissibility of a state which can use coercion for certain purposes, Nozick has to face a burden of showing that the redistribution of income and wealth is not a legitimate purpose for the state to pursue through coercion.

His attempt to do this is embodied in his defence of what he calls the 'entitlement' theory of justice in holdings, which will take up the rest of our discussion. The entitlement theory consists of three principles:

1   A person who acquires a holding in accordance with the principle of justice in acquisition is entitled to that holding.
2   A person who acquires a holding in accordance with the principle of justice in transfer, from someone else entitled to the holding, is entitled to the holding.
3   No-one is entitled to a holding except by (repeated) applications of 1 and 2 (Nozick 1974: 151).

Obviously, Nozick needs to say what counts as justice in acquisition and justice in transfer. But even before looking at what he has to say about those questions, we can see that the entitlement theory seems to have a different shape from the theories encountered in previous chapters. Rather than specifying a pattern of distribution to which the world has to conform, Nozick's theory specifies a set of procedures, the mere fulfilment of which guarantees justice. It is, he claims, a historical theory, in this sense: merely looking at the current distribution of resources, at who has what, tells us nothing about whether the distribution is just; we have to know how that distribution came to be, that is, whether the principles of justice in acquisition and in transfer have been followed. He opposes his theory to what he calls 'patterned' theories, like those of Rawls and other egalitarians. In patterned theories we can know whether justice is achieved simply by seeing whether the existing distribution fits the pattern specified by the principle of justice.

On, then, to Nozick's principles of justice in acquisition and in transfer. He states the principle of justice in acquisition as follows:

> A is entitled to X, if no-one else is entitled to X and if in taking X A does not make anyone else's condition worse (except in the competitive senses that they cannot use the resources that A has appropriated, and that A may be able to use those resources for his own advantage in a competitive market). (Nozick 1974: 177–8)

Nozick provides surprisingly little argument for the principle of justice in acquisition, focusing almost exclusively on the proviso (that A's taking X does not worsen the condition of others). He explicitly rejects theories of justice in acquisition, like John Locke's, that make acquisition depend on mixing labour with, or in some other way improving the value of, the object acquired. Ultimately the argument for the first part of the principle seems to be just that there is no reason to object to an original acquisition except that it leaves others worse off, and that exception is dealt with by the proviso.

That Nozick provides no argument for the principle is, perhaps surprisingly, not a serious criticism. The proponents of redistribution whom he treats as his main opponents also say very little about original acquisition. Obviously, someone who believed, for example, that the well-being of the earth mattered independently of its usefulness to human beings might argue against Nozick's principle on the grounds that it makes no reference to the interests of other beings than humans. But Nozick's redistributive opponents largely agree with him that human interests matter exclusively. Furthermore, even those who disagree about that are liable to concede it for the sake of argument: they want to argue with him about redistribution among humans, and so will focus on the principles he offers on the assumption that they try to capture what justice requires *in so far as* the interests of humans matter.

Far more contentious is Nozick's principle of justice in transfer:

> A transfer from A to — is just as long as A and — both consent to the transfer from A to — and neither is coerced. (Nozick 1974: 115)

Nozick does acknowledge that the proviso attached to the principle of justice in acquisition must, in principle, affect our judgements about the principle of justice in transfer. He says that 'some reflection of the proviso about appropriation constrains later actions' (Nozick 1974: 179). But these circumstances are very rare ('the proviso will (almost?) never come into effect', Nozick 1974: 179); only when someone appropriates enough of some commodity which is essential for life, and thus jeopardizes other people's survival, would the proviso kick in.

Nozick provides an argument for the principle of justice in transfer, which has the conclusion that any other principle, and in particular any redistributive taxation, would involve unwarranted interference in human liberty. He makes this argument with two compelling examples: the famous Wilt Chamberlain example and the less famous example of the movie-goer and the sunset-watcher. Let's start with the Wilt Chamberlain example. Suppose that Wilt Chamberlain is a highly talented and entertaining basketball player,[1] and signs a contract with his team specifying that in each home game he gets 25 cents from the price of every ticket sold, and that after 1 million fans have attended he has made $250,000 (Nozick wrote the book in 1974, which explains the paucity of the sum). Nozick's simple question is: 'is this new distribution unjust? If so, why?' (Nozick 1974: 161). After all, the fans have each voluntarily given their 25 cents to him; the team voluntarily contracted with Chamberlain to allow him to have the money; people who did not want to see Chamberlain play did not have to give anything up, and are all as well off as they were before the season began. No-one, Nozick thinks, has grounds for complaint:

> If the people were entitled to dispose of the resources to which they were entitled, didn't this include their being entitled to give it to, or exchange with, Wilt Chamberlain? Can anyone else complain on grounds of justice? . . . After someone transfers something to Wilt Chamberlain, third parties still have their legitimate shares; *their* shares are not changed. By what process could such a transfer among two persons give rise to a legitimate claim of distributive justice on a portion of what was transferred, by a third party who had no claim of justice

on any holding of the others *before* the transfer? (Nozick 1974: 161–2)

But to reinstate a pattern would require coercive redistribution. Patterns require coercion for their stability – that is, a violation of the prohibition on aggression. But the principle 'from each as they choose, to each as they are chosen' requires no coercion, and so is compatible with the prohibition on aggression against persons.

Nozick's second example concerns a comparison between two people, one of whom likes to watch sunsets, and the other of whom can achieve the same level of satisfaction or flourishing only by going to movies. The sunset-watcher has no need for money to achieve his enjoyment – he just needs to be awake and sighted at the relevant moment and in suitable weather conditions. But the movie-goer has to earn money through paid work in order to get the same satisfaction. Suppose the movie ticket costs $8 and the movie-goer has an $8/hour job. Without taxation the movie-goer would have to work for an hour to acquire the price of a ticket, but suppose that the tax rate is 25 per cent. Then in order to earn $8 the movie-goer must work about fifteen minutes more than an hour: that is, fifteen minutes more than he would have had to work in the absence of coercive taxation. But the sunset-watcher has no additional burden: he continues to get his satisfaction free.

> Why should we treat the man whose happiness requires certain material goods or services differently from the man whose preferences and desires make such goods unnecessary for his happiness? Why should the man who prefers seeing a movie (and who has to earn money for a ticket) be open to the required call to aid the needy, while the person who prefers looking at a sunset (and hence need earn no extra money) is not? Indeed, isn't it surprising that redistributionists choose to ignore the man whose pleasures are so easily attainable without extra labor, while adding yet another burden to the poor unfortunate who must work for his pleasures? (Nozick 1974: 170)

The comparison is supposed to support the claim that taxation is 'on a par with forced labour', that is, on a par with a moderate form of slavery (Nozick 1974: 169).

The Wilt Chamberlain example is supposed to demonstrate both that multiple bilateral transactions will inevitably lead to unequal outcomes, and that redistribution away from the distributions arrived at by the market will require 'continual interference' (Nozick 1974: 163) in the lives of the agents concerned. In order to maintain a pattern (whether equality, equality of opportunity, maximin or any other predetermined goal), the state must monitor all economic activity, and interfere to frustrate the aims of the agents. The movie-goer example is supposed to build on this intuition, and show how redistribution afflicts the life of the person who is taxed: they are forced to do more work than they would otherwise have to in order to achieve their ends.

What could be wrong with the distribution arrived at after a year of people paying to see Wilt Chamberlain play basketball? Nozick emphasizes the transparent nature of the transaction by having the fans place the 25 cents which goes to Chamberlain in a separate box, and the transaction is clearly voluntary. The people who do not go to see Chamberlain are not made worse off, so no non-consenting person's situation is worsened by the transaction. What could be objectionable?

It is not so clear, though, that no-one's situation is worsened by the transaction. Third parties are often affected significantly by bilateral transactions, and it is reasonable to expect that non-consenting others will have their situations worsened in a number of ways. First, inequality itself may affect people who live in an unequal society. There is evidence, for example, that health outcomes for people who live in an unequal society are worse than for those who live at the same absolute level of wealth but in a less unequal society (Wilkinson 1996). Being on the receiving end of an inequality may involve loss of social status that makes one worse off, all things considered, than if one had the same level of wealth in a more equal society. Second, wealth influences who has political power. Prior to the emergence of inequality in Nozick's story, no-one had more wealth with which to influence political outcomes than anyone else. After the emergence of inequality, Chamberlain has more wealth, and so suddenly has more power (potentially) than the third parties, who are no worse off financially than before, but suddenly may be worse off politically. Third, there may be goods which, although the non-basketball fans have no less money, they are less likely to be able to afford (so that their money is worth less to them). Some goods are absolutely scarce, so that, assuming constant demand, what enables someone to have access to them is just having more money than others. For example, there are only so many people who can own second homes in an unspoilt area of Vermont. If more than that number own second homes, the good – an unspoilt area – is compromised, and no-one can have it. Once a wealthy class of people emerges, members of that class will be able to crowd out others from this good who previously might have afforded it, even though those others are no less wealthy than before.

Finally, there are many non-consenting others whose prospects are affected by the emergence of inequality: the children of all the participants in the economy. Wilt Chamberlain's children can have superior educational opportunities, and will be left more money than the children of either the basketball fans or the non-fans, and so will have more prospects for getting access to the goods which society agrees to distributing unequally. If equality of opportunity in the next generation matters at all, that is a reason for thinking there is at least something wrong with the outcome of the transaction.

So there are several reasons for thinking that the outcome of the transaction might be partially flawed. These reasons might be overridden if, as Nozick suggests, the taxation required to correct for them – that is, to compensate others for the bads produced for them by the outcome – required continual interference in the lives of economic agents. He says that 'no end-state principle or distributional patterned principle of justice can be continuously realized without continuous interference with people's lives' (Nozick 1974: 163). Is this true? It is certainly true that if the aim was to ensure that at no point did anyone have more resources than anyone else, the state would have a lot of work to do. It would have to enforce a prohibition on all transactions that left some people better off than others, and this would be a Herculean task, as well as one the implementation of which would involve very high levels of intrusion into people's lives. But this objection afflicts only theories which object to any significant departures from equality at any given time. As we have seen, most egalitarian theories are not like this: they allow for significant inequalities of resources to persist, and are sensitive to the costs of state intrusion into people's everyday lives. Because egalitarians place a high priority on the basic liberties, they will straightforwardly rule out redistributive mechanisms that violate those liberties. But the standard mechanism available in contemporary capitalist societies, the tax–benefit system, is not experienced as an intrusion in people's everyday lives. Money is taken out of the paycheque, and a form is filled in toward the end of the financial year. Increasing the marginal rate of taxation increases the extent of taxation, but does not increase the extent to which people's lives are intruded into. And remember from our discussion of Friedman that maintaining private property rights itself involves the government in having a large coercive apparatus. Taxation is no more coercive than policing to maintain private property, and no more intrusive into people's pursuit of their own paths in life.

But is taxation, nevertheless, 'on a par with forced labor' (Nozick 1974: 169), as the movie-goer example suggests? Even if taxation is not, and is not experienced as, a deep intrusion into someone's life, that it is relevantly like forced labour in a moral sense is a damning charge. But it is one that, I think, can be resisted. First, think of one major difference between the sunset-watcher and movie-goer. The sunset-watcher gets his satisfaction from nature, from regarding a natural phenomenon that was produced without any human effort. The movie-goer, by contrast, is participating in a social world. The means of his satisfaction is produced by talented technicians, actors, artists, writers, producers, whose talents were developed in part through a system of social investment (schooling, parenting, etc.), who are all responding to complex constellations of incentives, economic and non-economic. The sunset-watcher is enjoying something which is really free; the movie-goer is deeply dependent on others. The taxation could reasonably be seen as a contribution to maintaining the social framework required to continue reproducing the means of his satisfaction.

Whether or not that is true, I think it is wrong to think of the movie-goer as being forced (or treated in a way that is equivalent to being forced) to work. The movie-goer has an array of possible sources of satisfaction, many of which are free: sunset-watching comes to mind. He is not forced to go to the movie: it is something he wants to do, and he has to labour in order to do it. Nozick does not deny this, but he says that the taxation forces him to labour longer than he would otherwise have to. Certainly, as long as other people are not being taxed, the movie-goer can say this. But Nozick is not defending the claim that this particular person is being forced to work, but that all people who are subject to taxation are being forced to labour longer than they would otherwise have to for the same return. But there is simply no reason to believe this. What return we get on our labour depends not only on how much effort we put in and how much talent we have, but also on how the natural and social environment is arranged. Who knows what return each would be getting on their labour if no-one were being taxed? To imagine that counterfactual is to imagine a world very far removed from our own. Maybe in such a world there would be no infrastructural support for the particular market in which the person works, and his labour would bring him only a subsistence living. Perhaps not: we need much more information than Nozick can provide before we can have any confidence in his assertion.

Conclusion

Focusing on freedom and entitlement does not seem a promising way of blocking the case for redistribution. But Nozick evinces and Friedman explicitly elaborates a concern that governments frequently act against the goals of justice. Libertarians alert us to a serious practical problem, which is how best to design constitutional measures to assure that the power they are granted to enforce justice will not be used to commit injustices or other bads. While I have expressed scepticism about the strength of Friedman's pessimistic induction that non-capitalist states excessively encroach on freedom, I think the least that theorists of justice should take away from the libertarian critique of redistribution is an appreciation of the difficulties involved in designing states to deliver justice.

6
Justice and Groups

In the preceding chapters I have assumed what I call ethical individualism – the idea that individual persons are the sole ultimate objects of moral concern. All of the theorists we have looked at are concerned only that individuals receive what is justly theirs, whether this is resources, opportunities, liberties or freedom. All the theorists talk of rights, and all of them mean individual rights: protections of individual interests that neither the state nor other individuals can be justified in violating.

But some people claim that the injustices they suffer are not reducible to violations of individuals' rights. Some injustices are injustices to whole peoples, or groups of people. The way that slavery was carried out in the United States, for example, did indeed involve the violation of individuals' rights to self-ownership, but was not reducible to that: a wrong was done to the group as a whole. In this chapter I want to explore two ways of vindicating the claim that particular groups have rights, the violation of which constitutes injustice. Both start from the premise that it is individuals who count, ultimately, but they depart in both their argumentative strategy and the kinds of group-based rights they license.

Kymlicka's liberal theory of group-differentiated rights

Will Kymlicka has developed a highly influential revision of liberal theory in the light of communitarian critiques, one which claims that the liberal theory of justice should recognize that, although individuals are ultimately what matter, they are not the only entities that can have rights. In fact, he argues, egalitarian liberals of the Rawlsian kind should advocate what he calls group-differentiated rights. In the rest of this chapter I shall outline his argument and some of its implications, and then examine some of the responses to it.

The central argument proceeds in two stages. First, Kymlicka argues that membership of a cultural community should count as a primary good (in the Rawlsian sense of a good that any rational person would want whatever else she wanted), and then that its status as a primary good justifies some special cultural rights and protections which conflict with and override some standard liberal rights.

The first stage of the argument proceeds by analogy with Rawls's argument for the Liberty Principle (see pp. 61–5). Rawls identifies self-respect as a good crucial to the ability to pursue our conception of the good whatever that is. But we can only have self-respect, and the confidence in ourselves and conception of the good which accompanies it, if we have a conception of the good with which we can identify. In turn, this requires that we enjoy the conditions in which we can realistically form and revise our beliefs about how to live. This interest in the capacity to form and revise our conception of the good supports the Liberty Principle; in particular it supports very firm guarantees for freedom of expression, freedom of association and freedom of conscience.

But, Kymlicka adds, the ability to form and revise our conception of the good is not just dependent on our own capacities and guarantees of freedom. It also depends on there being background cultural and intellectual institutions which we can realistically draw on in developing our beliefs. We do not spontaneously form our beliefs about the good life – we take up and subject to scrutiny and revision the ideas which surround us. The background culture, in other words, provides a 'context of choice' without which the liberty to form and revise our conception of the good is empty, in the sense that it cannot serve the interest which justifies it. Thus, the cultural structure provides a context of choice which is essential for self-respect (Kymlicka 1989: 166; 1995: 82–4). So membership in a cultural structure is a primary good in much the same way as are some of the basic liberties protected by the Liberty Principle.

It is important that this argument is true to traditional liberalism in that it is entirely individualistic in form. It does not assert the primacy of group interests over individual interests, or any obligation of the individual to subjugate his or her interests to those of the group to which he or she happens to belong. Group membership is recognized to be in some strong sense morally arbitrary. Instead, Kymlicka asserts the importance to each individual of a cultural context of choice for 'pursuing our essential interest in living a good life' (Kymlicka 1989: 165). The interest in autonomy, understood quite strongly, is asserted to support a strong interest in cultural membership.

The mere fact that people have an interest in cultural membership does not suffice to justify any special rights. The second stage of Kymlicka's argument, however, tries to establish that there are indeed special rights or protections supported by this interest, and that when they conflict with standard liberal rights they sometimes take precedence. The argument proceeds as follows:

- For liberals the interests of each member of the community matter equally (Kymlicka 1989: 182–3).
- Egalitarian political and economic procedures (constitutional democracy and constrained markets) *generally* support outcomes which are fair in the sense that they count each individual's interests equally (Kymlicka 1989: 183).
- But small cultural communities can be outbid in markets and outvoted in majoritarian democracies on matters which are crucial to their survival as a cultural community (Kymlicka 1989; 183).[1] They can be outbid in markets because there are important economies of scale attached to the production of mass culture, and because

there are powerful incentives for creators of culture to aim for large audiences. A Hollywood movie costs $100 million to make, quite apart from distribution costs: it is simply implausible that such a movie made in Slovenian, or Welsh, will make back its costs, because only a handful of Slovenian or Welsh speakers will watch it. Similarly, if a popular singing group wants to make a great deal of money – or even have its work understood and appreciated by a large audience – it will avoid writing songs in a language understood only by a few hundred thousand people.[2]

- The liberal theory of equality supports claims based on *unequal circumstances* but not on *differential choices*. So any special rights claim must be grounded in the former and not in the latter (Kymlicka 1989: 185–6).
- But aboriginal special rights claims *can* be based in unequal circumstances, because the choices of surrounding cultures render, say, the survival of aboriginal languages vulnerable in a way that is not reciprocal (Kymlicka 1989: 187).

Therefore, according to Kymlicka, there will be circumstances in which the liberal principle that individuals should be compensated for their unequal circumstances justifies recognizing group rights over culture.

One difficulty in evaluating Kymlicka's argument is that the obvious real-world cases to which his argument might be thought to apply are ones where the potential recipients of the group right are people who are currently living with the unjust legacy of past infractions of (non-group-regarding) liberal principles of justice. So, for example, American Indians have been subjected over the past few centuries to acts of genocide; within living memory they were segregated by law from white Americans, and hence rendered unable to integrate; and, as sovereign nations, they have signed coerced treaties with the US Federal government on which the latter subsequently reneged.[3] It is true that all these evils were done to individuals, most of whom are no longer alive (and who wouldn't be alive now even if the wrong done to them had not been that of killing them). But it is hard to believe that the high rates of alcoholism, the low educational achievement levels and the low life expectancy and expected lifetime incomes of American Indians are entirely unconnected with these wrongs. Contemporary American Indians are living with current injustice that is the result of past violations of liberal justice. As a matter of rectificatory justice, many liberals will say that group-differentiated rights would be morally acceptable (although they might argue that such rights will be *ineffective* in addressing these injustices, and hence should be rejected, but only because they are ineffective, not because they violate liberal norms as a matter of principle). Most liberal defenders of affirmative action, for example, take this view (see Dworkin 1985: chs 14–15).

Kymlicka's appeal to the possibility that minorities will be outvoted in constitutional democratic procedures might suggest that he is not departing from the mainstream liberal view as much as he, in fact, is. He says they might be 'outvoted on matters crucial to their survival as a cultural community', and the examples he gives are 'crucial policy decisions (e.g. on what language will be used, or whether public works programs will support or conflict with aboriginal work patterns)' (Kymlicka 1989: 183). But it is hard to believe that these kinds of example frequently jeopardize cultural survival unless either they are themselves violations of standard liberal injustice or the culture has already been rendered vulnerable by past violations of liberal justice. So, for example, denying people the right to a trial in their native tongue would violate the right to due process, and forbidding them from speaking in their native tongue would violate the right to freedom of expression. Work patterns are not essential to the character of a culture, and a robust culture, the members of which have a variety of economic opportunities, can adjust to new work patterns (as Christians have, perhaps regrettably, changed their attitude toward the Sabbath during the growth of capitalism). A culture threatened by decisions about work patterns which do not violate standard liberal justice is already in jeopardy, and in our world this has usually been due to a history like that described above.

But Kymlicka is *not* advancing group-differentiated rights merely as a matter of rectificatory justice. He is offering them as a solution to an ongoing condition that would, he thinks, be a matter of justice even if no violations of standard individual rights had occurred in the past.

He makes this clear with his shipwreck example, a modification of Ronald Dworkin's initial auction, which I shall quote at length:[4]

> Two ships, one very large and one quite small, shipwreck on an island, and to ensure a smooth auction, they proceed by entering bids into the ships' computers without ever leaving the ship. . . . The auction proceeds and it turns out that the passengers of the two ships are very similar in the distribution of ways of life chosen. . . . Finally the resources are all bid for, but when they disembark from the ship they discover for the first time, what had been obscured by the use of a common computer language, that the two ships are of different nationalities. Assuming, as is reasonable, that their resources are distributed evenly across the island, they will now be forced to try to execute their chosen lifestyles in an alien culture – e.g. in their work, and, when the state superstructure is built, in the courts, schools, legislatures, etc. (Kymlicka 1989: 188)[5]

The disadvantage faced by members of the minority nation is that the majority members 'possess and utilize their resources within a certain context, i.e. within their own cultural community' (Kymlicka 1989: 188) whereas the minority members have to utilize their resources within a cultural community which is not their own. In the absence of other special measures designed to protect their culture, they would have to purchase and settle a separate part of the island to secure their cultural community – and this is an extra 'cost which members of the majority community do not incur, but which in no way reflects different choices about the good life (or about the importance of cultural membership within it)' (Kymlicka 1989: 189).

There is no history of standard liberal injustices to rectify here. The thought experiment is supposed to show that special measures can be justified not only for purposes of rectification, but also as measures which are, in themselves, required by justice – in particular by the standard liberal conception of equality.

It is worth noting that for Kymlicka the notion of a secure cultural context of choice is, fairly clearly, a threshold notion. Were the minority culture secure, there would be no case for redistribution, even if fewer resources were being devoted to the culture than to the majority culture. Security is all that is needed. How much it takes to secure a culture will depend on the circumstances, including the ability of proponents of other cultures to reach into the minority culture and attract supporters from it.

Kymlicka can be criticized from two main directions. Some theorists argue that, even though he advocates group rights, he still fails to recognize the deep sense in which persons are constituted by their communities. From the other side are theorists who argue that in so far as there are wrongs that emanate from unequal membership of cultures, standard individual rights suffice to deal with them.

How would the first kind of criticism go? Unlike the other theorists of justice we have discussed so far, Kymlicka explicitly identifies cultural resources as playing a vital role in promoting individual flourishing, and so believes that when a culture is under threat it needs to be supported for the sake of the individuals who need its resources. However, like the other liberals, he believes that these resources only contribute to individual flourishing if the individual endorses from the inside, as it were, the way that she is living her life, and he claims that individual interests are the justification for group rights. So although Kymlicka is more sensitive than other liberals to the contribution of culture to flourishing, and advocates different policy outcomes, he shares with them a deep individualism, and the idea that our communities do not have a distinctive claim on us, let alone constitute us.

Second, there is a difficulty with the first stage of Kymlicka's argument: the claim that a cultural context of choice is needed for individual autonomy. This claim seems true, but partly because it is not clear what it would be to lack a cultural context of choice in a society.[6] To take the most extreme case, a monolingual individual moves to a foreign culture which deploys a foreign language. She lives within a cultural context which sets the background for her choices. She brings with her internal personal resources informed by her own culture. *That* culture, of course, is no longer reinforced by her daily experiences, but a new culture does interact with her own culture to give meaning and content to her choices.

I do not mean to underestimate the extreme difficulties facing the person whose situation I have described – of course, she faces a massive set of disadvantages which it is entirely unreasonable to expect any but the most robust and cheerful personalities to deal with well. But the point is that even in this case it is not clear that the person lacks a cultural context of choice. And if she doesn't lack a cultural context of choice, it is not clear what lacking a cultural context of choice means.

Suppose that the idea of lacking a cultural context of choice makes sense. The main difficulty with Kymlicka's argument for group-differentiated rights comes from the fact that the design of institutions has a dynamic effect on the reproduction of culture. The shipwreck case looks plausible as long as we consider culture to be static and relevant only to the adults landing on the island. But instituting special rights will affect how the two cultures develop, how the relationship between them develops, and which cultures the children of the shipwreck survivors will opt for. Suppose a set of special rights designed to protect the minority culture is implemented, and is successful. The survivors themselves will then be able to live out their lives in their original culture. But such rights may also support the culture artificially by channelling the survivors' children into it. The most obvious case is that of special language rights – say, allowing parents to send their children to schools in which all subjects are taught in the minority language, and providing through public funds a minority-language TV and radio service. If children do not learn the majority language as children, they will have great difficulty entering the majority culture as adults. But suppose that the majority economy contains a more diverse set of opportunities than the minority economy. Then the children of the minority have available to them fewer economic opportunities than the children of the majority. Equal opportunity for the children is compromised in favour of the cultural membership of the parents.

An example, slightly adapted from reality, makes this vivid. Today Welsh is a minority language even in Wales. But it was not always so. One hundred and fifty years ago the vast majority of inhabitants of Wales were Welsh-speakers, most of them monolingual. Yet Welsh was, even then, a language spoken by very few people, compared with English. In fact, English was forced on the Welsh by comparatively mild violations of liberal justice – it was prohibited from schools and courts, setting up distorted incentives for parents to force their children to learn English. But suppose, counterfactually, that no such violations of liberal justice had occurred, and that special language rights, of the kinds that have recently been granted, had been granted in the late nineteenth century. Many young people who currently grow up speaking only English or both English and Welsh would have grown up instead as monolingual Welsh speakers. They would have had far fewer cultural and material opportunities than they do as English speakers. They would have realistic access to a much less diverse range of potential life-partners, to a much less rich body of literature, drama, scholarship and popular culture in their own language, and to a much less extensive and diverse range of well-paying and rewarding employment opportunities. In short, the mild violations of liberal justice made these people much better off than they would have been in the presence of the special rights Kymlicka recommends.

Kymlicka understands that other strictures of liberal justice will sometimes conflict with the special cultural rights he recommends (Kymlicka 1989: 194–7). He places a premium on the liberal individual freedoms which protect the individual's ability rationally to reflect on and to revise her conception of the good life, since these are preconditions for living a good life: 'Liberals can and should endorse certain external protections where they promote fairness between groups, but should reject internal restrictions which limit the right of group members to question and revise traditional authorities and practices' (Kymlicka 1995: 37; see also 1989: 81–2). But beyond that there is no reason, for Kymlicka, to suppose that standard liberal prescriptions always, or even normally, take precedence over the special rights justified by his equality argument.

There are two problems here. First, our ability to revise our practices and question authority depends crucially on what other opportunities are available to us. If I have a realistic option of exiting Culture A to Culture B that not only establishes another option for me outside Culture A, but also generally establishes for me a more diverse range of options within Culture A, the traditional authorities have more incentive to bend to my demands for revision in order to keep me within Culture A. The degree of permeability of boundaries between cultures affects what goes on within them, including the extent to which members of cultures can be restricted. This fact compromises Kymlicka's crucial distinction between *internal restrictions* (designed to protect a culture from the recalcitrant choices of its members) and *external protections* (designed to protect the culture from the choices of non-members). If the interest in having conditions in which we can exercise our capacity rationally to reconsider and revise our conception of the good supports an interest in cultural membership, it also supports an interest in having permeable boundaries between our culture and other cultures. But the permeability of boundaries will predictably be limited by many special rights, in particular by language rights. If, for example, special group language rights lead to more children growing up as monolingual speakers of the minority language, especially if the minority culture is itself illiberal, this limits their opportunities for exit, and thus their ability to reshape their home culture in their own interests.

The second problem is that many of those children whose futures will be shaped by group-differentiated rights are, like their parents, already on the receiving end of standard liberal injustices. For the most part, in the United States, Australia and other countries which feature heavily in Kymlicka's discussion, the liberal injustices they face are not primarily violations of the liberties which protect the ability to choose how to live and the interest in being able to revise one's choices, but they are the injustices of unequal resources and unequal material opportunities. If these inequalities are not only not corrected, but actually compounded by special rights, those special rights should be viewed with considerable suspicion. Consider the example of American Indians who live in communities which are allowed to prohibit sales of land and houses to persons who are not blood-members of the tribe. Such measures dramatically restrict the potential market for those homes and land, thus artificially reducing the actual and potential wealth of persons who already have less wealth than justice would demand. Some Welsh local councils are pressing for the right to double-tax homes owned as second homes, which would have a much lesser, but similar, effect on the wealth of homeowners who might want to move.

Margalit and Halbertal's personality-centred argument

Avishai Margalit and Moshe Halbertal have advanced an alternative to Kymlicka's argument which would, in principle, support a set of group-related policies more amenable to communitarians. Like Kymlicka, they start with the interests of individuals, and argue for group rights on those grounds. However, they give much greater weight in conceptualizing the interests of individuals than Kymlicka does to belonging to a particular group. They start with the importance of what they call 'personality identity', which captures what is important in the concept of the anthropological individual: 'The same person can undergo a radical change in personality yet remain the same person, whereas the converse is not the case. Culture plays a crucial role in shaping the personalities of individuals, especially in those aspects that they and their environment consider central for constituting their personality identity' (Margalit and Halbertal 1994: 501–2). Individuals thus have a morally powerful interest in preserving the conditions which make for security of their personality identity. But cultural environment plays a crucial role in making for such stability. Were the culture to change dramatically, or were individuals deprived of the cultural context in which they were accustomed to operating, their personality identity would be threatened, made insecure. So, according to Margalit and Halbertal, individuals have a right to their own culture.

It should be obvious that this right to one's own culture can support claims to more extensive government action than the mere benign neglect that liberalism traditionally requires. Margalit and Halbertal identify two levels of the right to culture, and say that their main aim is to vindicate a third.

The first level is the 'right to maintain a comprehensive way of life within the larger society without interference' (Margalit and Halbertal 1994: 497). This is the traditional liberal stance of benign neglect toward culture: the state does not interfere deliberately with the ability of individuals (whether alone, or in concert with others) to pursue their cultural goals, except in so far as this is an unavoidable side-effect of other activities the state is committed to (for example, protecting the rights of others, or engaging in coercive taxation). The second level adds 'the right to recognition of the community's way of life by the general society' (Margalit and Halbertal 1994: 498). This right does not call on the state to do more than the first, but does call upon other people in the society to act without contempt and disdain toward others on the grounds of their membership of a culture. The third, and most demanding, level adds 'the right to support for the way of life by the state's institutions so that the culture can flourish' (Margalit and Halbertal 1994: 498).

This third level of support involves the redistribution of resources from members of secure cultures to support the underlying sources of stability for less secure cultures: 'In our example of the Ultra-Orthodox culture this means financial support for Torah institutions and Torah scholars, which is a crucial condition for the culture's flourishing' (Margalit and Halbertal 1994: 499). Member cultures of a state have a claim on the state (and therefore on both their own members and the members of other cultures) for support for activities that sustain them. This makes sense: if someone has a right to their own culture, then they have a right to the resources that are necessary to make that culture available, but have no right to spend the resources made available for that purpose on anything else (like, for example, participating in a different culture, or a new car).

How does this view differ from Kymlicka's? Kymlicka believes that we each have a right to culture, but not necessarily to the culture in which we were raised (our 'own' culture). So whereas Kymlicka's view implies that sometimes we should respond to a catastrophic decline in a culture by trying to ease the transition of those individuals affected into another culture, Margalit and Halbertal will place great weight on the importance of maintaining the culture in decline. Margalit and Halbertal's view, in addition, is more openly amenable to the idea that we should sometimes protect groups even when doing so conflicts with the individual rights of members of those groups.

Three considerations count strongly against Margalit and Halbertal's view. The first two work against their particular argument for group rights: that cultures evolve, and people are extremely adaptable. The third afflicts all group rights views, and concerns the actual costs to individuals of protecting group rights, so I shall take that up separately in chapter 8.

The central problems with Margalit and Halbertal's argument for the right to one's own culture are that cultures evolve and people are adaptable. To take the first point: cultures evolve often as a result of the unintended consequences of practices that take place within the culture, and changes in material conditions over which nobody has any real control. British culture was different in 1998 from how it was in 1958, and only partly because of the introduction of members of different cultures to British life. Yet nobody could have foreseen the cultural changes, at least in any detail.

But government aid to a culture, if it is to be effective, has to be guided by some picture of how the culture is or should be. If government aid is forthcoming to some minority culture, it will inevitably affect the development of the culture. Usually the effects will be conservative: the aim, after all, on Margalit and Halbertal's view, is to preserve the culture, and since the natural direction of the culture is so hard to gauge, the government will be guided by the current content of the culture. But this action takes the direction of the culture, to some extent, out of the hands of the members of the culture. Furthermore, within any culture, there are disagreements about the true content of the culture. In aiding the culture with a particular vision of it in mind, the government must of necessity take sides on these disagreements. It will thus be strengthening a particular vision of the culture against the wishes of some of the members of that very culture.

It is worth commenting here that material and regulatory support for a particular culture is always coercive, and is often coercive of members of that culture. Margalit and

Halbertal suggest apparently harmless measures such as funding Torah scholarship, but the funding has to come from somewhere, and it will typically come from coercive taxation, which will often have been imposed on Orthodox Jews themselves (among others).

Along similar lines David Miller advocates support for a national culture, arguing that 'very often this [protection of the national culture] can be done by inducements rather than by coercion: farmers can be given incentives to preserve their hedgerows; the domestic film industry can be subsidized out of cinema revenues; important works of art can be purchased for national collections; and so forth' (Miller 1995: 88). But the mechanisms he describes *are* coercive. Certainly, they do not coerce the farmer and the broadcast company owner; instead they coerce the cinema-goer and the taxpayer. Even regulation which does not directly redistribute resources can restrict the freedom of members of the protected culture to live their lives by their own lights, and thus both coerces them and constrains the free development of the culture itself. A famous example is Quebec's Bill 101 (passed in 1977), which requires, among other things, that all companies which employ more than fifty people must function in French, and that all commercial and road signs must be in French only, and which limits the access to anglophone schooling for all children. These measures do, of course, immediately affect the behaviour primarily of anglophone citizens, but francophone citizens are not exempt: they, too, have to send their children to francophone schools, whether they want to or not, and to use French in their business operations, whether they want to or not.

People are, furthermore, quite adaptable. Because cultures evolve and change, they have to be, if their personality identities are to be secure. There are many changes in circumstances, some tragic (loss of spouses, parents, children, friends), others less so (loss of jobs, changes in working conditions, changes in job shifts, relocations), which people regularly bear with fortitude. The *gradual* change of, or even disappearance of, a minority culture, which is the worst we would expect to occur if the standard liberal stance toward culture were maintained by the state, may be a hurdle for someone to overcome, but it seems extravagant to claim that people will lose their personalities as a result of it. The case of sudden catastrophic disappearance of a culture may, of course, be different. But, in the rare cases where this will happen within liberal democracies (I cannot think of a single actual example), there seems to be as strong a case that the government should provide resources to smooth the transition for the individuals involved as there does for the government to try to maintain the culture artificially.

Conclusion

I have cast doubt on the justifications of group-based protections by emphasizing two points. First, cultures are rarely under real threat from genuinely liberal institutions, and when they are, it is usually due to the choices of members of those cultures; so the rights to culture are actually rights to control the choice-making of other people, who, by definition, do not endorse their own membership of the culture. Second, minorities are not homogeneous: they contain minorities within them, and group-based protections tend to benefit primarily those who already have most power within the minority.

I find the arguments against Margalit and Halbertal's support for very strong group protections compelling. Kymlicka's position is less demanding, and more resistant to the objections I have surveyed. His claim is that there is no reason *in principle* to reject group protections, as long as those protections can be put in place without jeopardizing individual liberties, or can be shown to benefit individuals at least as much as the reductions in individual liberties they might involve. The sceptical objections developed above do not challenge the claim of principle so much as to say that when there have been no violations of liberal justice more standardly conceived, Kymlicka's conditions will not be met.

7

Affirmative Action, Equality of Opportunity and the Gendered Division of Labour

Despite occasional discussions of practical matters, I've devoted most of my attention so far to explaining the competing theories of justice and evaluating the arguments in their favour. In this chapter we shall look at how the theories we have encountered deal with a series of contemporary political problems. Remember from the discussion of reflective equilibrium (chapter 2) that it matters for evaluation of the theories how well they deal with particular cases or problems. On some matters our intuitions are so firm that conflicting with them is extremely powerful evidence against a theory, however meticulous the abstract justification of the theory appears. Consider slavery. This is, for most of us, just not up for discussion: if we discovered of a purported theory of justice that it licensed slavery in many different kinds of circumstances, we would find it drained of intuitive appeal. Of course, there is a pervasive moral consensus against slavery, so it may not be surprising that we give our intuitions about it great authority. But, among controversial issues, I think abortion may be one about which many people feel the same way. Many opponents and many defenders of the right to abortion will look for a theory's implications for the right to abortion. If it finds their own view about abortion wanting, they will, automatically, also find it wanting.

But, as the method of reflective equilibrium insists, our intuitions about cases are not always decisive, and it may be a virtue of a theory that, although it finds against our intuitions on an issue, it does so in a way that explains to us why our intuition is mistaken, or, at least, should be questioned. I'm going to test the theories we have looked at against three particular issues. For each of these issues I assume that most readers will have formed views, but also that their intuitions are not as firm as they are regarding slavery or (perhaps) abortion. My aim is less to show you that one or another theory deals better with a given issue than it is to illustrate how to look at real social issues through a theoretical prism, and how to use thinking about an issue to guide reflection on a theory.

The first is the issue of affirmative action. Affirmative action covers a collection of methods for making reparation to people who either are now the victims of injustice or are relevantly related to people who were, in the past, victims of injustice. In the United States, affirmative action has been applied to racial and ethnic minorities and also to women. The least demanding forms of affirmative action require employers and universities to post information about their openings widely, to ensure that members of the targeted groups are likely to be aware of the opportunities available to them. More demanding forms give weight to membership of the targeted group in deciding whether an individual will be hired or admitted to the college; the most demanding of all (which are very rare) set quotas for the members of targeted groups by saying, for example, that at least 10 per cent of an entering class must be African-American, or at least 40 per cent must be women. In public life in the United States, oddly enough, the prevailing justification of affirmative action is not justice-based, but defends it as a public good. But the most compelling justifications are justice-based, and my interest is going to be in the different stances the theories I describe take toward it.

The second issue concerns equal opportunity and the family. To what extent is it objectionable that society allows parents to pass advantages on to their children? It is curious that in the United States, where only 0.5 per cent of the population is wealthy enough to pay the estate tax (a tax imposed on estates worth over $1 million at a person's death), a large majority of respondents to opinion polls favour the abolition of the tax. When respondents are told some simple facts about the tax – that it is easy to avoid; that much of the wealth it taxes is a capital gain that has not previously been taxed; that it only starts at over $1 million, and contains a wealth of exemptions – many switch to opposing abolition, but a majority remain against the tax. My guess is that similar, but much more stringent, taxes in other democracies enjoy more support, but most people think there are various other ways in which it is permissible for parents to confer advantages on their children, even though there is no sense in which the children deserve the advantages they thereby enjoy. How we are raised (and whom we are born to) influences not only how much money is spent on us and how much we inherit, but also what our talents are and how they are developed, our propensity to exert effort, our educational opportunities and achievements, and our attitude toward particular risks. These all, in turn, influence how well off we are in our lives. Rawls's idea of fair equality of opportunity requires that, within the limits set by the priority of the Liberty Principle, people with the same level of talent and willingness to exert effort should face roughly similar prospects for resources and culture. But in existing wealthy democracies, fair equality of opportunity is far from realized. Class origin remains a good predictor of class destination, whether class is conceived of as household income level or as occupation type of head of household. Some of the mechanisms producing inequality of opportunity, we presume, are permitted by justice, but not necessarily all of them. The government does nothing wrong when it prohibits a parent from using her money to bribe a judge to get her daughter off a drugs charge; a university does nothing wrong when it turns down a candidate who is not quite qualified and thereby forfeits a large donation from the candidate's father. It may also be that a government does nothing wrong when it provides tax-funded compulsory schooling so that all children have at least a basic level of literacy and numeracy regardless of their parents' ability and inclination to pay.

The final issue concerns the gendered division of labour. In all countries, including all existing mature democracies, the labour market has a gendered aspect to it, and the tasks of domestic life are also vastly unequally shared between men and women. Men are paid more for the same work outside the home, and tend to predominate in the higher paid, more prestigious jobs; on top of that, they do less childcare and less household labour than the women they are married to, even if the latter work longer hours and bring in more money outside the home. In her book *The Second Shift* (1989), sociologist Arlie Hochschild in fact finds that in households where women earn more than their husbands, the domestic labour is even more unequally shared. Women who decide to absent themselves temporarily from the labour market in order to care for young children sacrifice not only the income they would have earned in those years, but also occupational and state retirement contributions and promotion opportunities, and, of course, for the rest of their working lives they experience the knock-on effect of not receiving raises during their years of absence. One American journalist estimates that her decision to stay home and care for her son in his infant and toddler years cost her over $600,000; her husband's earning power, by contrast, remained exactly as it would have been had he never had a son. Consider, too, that about 50 per cent of marriages in the United States end in divorce rather than death, and it is easy to see why, in an environment in which women take responsibility for this sort of labour, divorce typically worsens women's standards of living considerably, but hardly affects men's standards of living at all.

The figure of $600,000 is, of course, socially constructed. That is, different social arrangements would lead to a different figure. A policy which forced spouses with children to pool all their social security and pension contributions is possible; and it is feasible to have a law regulating divorce so that all parties have their standards of living affected identically until the youngest child reaches the age of majority (i.e., so that the divorced spouses have to pool their incomes until their children reach majority). Even that policy, though, would not overcome the inequality of impact on a couple's lifetime incomes as a result of their collective choice about who should be the carer in the child's early years. Some European countries (notably France and Sweden) have policies which lead to much less inequality in terms of standards of living than in the United States, though only Sweden has noticeably more egalitarian norms concerning the distribution of domestic chores. Other feasible arrangements could worsen the inequalities: if the US Social Security Administration did not have a rule that forces divorcing spouses who have been married more than twelve years to pool their social security contributions for their married years, women would be even worse off post-divorce, and hence their condition within a marriage would be less equal.

But the question here is this: does justice require the government to attend to these kinds of inequalities, and if so, in what ways is it permissible for the government to address them? Some theories of justice regard the inequalities both inside and outside the home as unjust; others consider neither to be unjust; still others object to the inequalities outside the home, but not to those inside the home. Now, it should be said that on all the theories we are considering, what the proper explanation is of the inequalities has some bearing on whether they are unjust or not. For most of the accounts, if the inequalities in the labour market were simply a reflection of natural differences between men and women, or were simply a reflection of autonomous choices that men and women made in the face of equal opportunity sets, then they would not count as unjust. However, in our world, this explanation is not a likely one, because we have ample evidence that the design of social institutions, as well as less concrete matters such as the prevailing norms in our culture, influence the decisions and choices men and women make, as well as the opportunity sets available to them. One other point to make is that most of the theories we have encountered have principled limits built into them on what may be done to change the division of labour in the home, even if it is unjust. In particular, most theories recognize some sort of private sphere, that is, that there are some limits to what the government may do to prevent people from acting on their own judgements about how to live. People's choices, even when we recognize that they are influenced by social norms and incentives, have a very strong claim to being respected by the state. In particular, coercive intervention in the home seems problematic. (Imagine a law telling people that over the course of the year each person in a home must clean the toilet no more than twice as often as anyone else in the home.) But intervention to readjust the division of labour in the home need not reach into the home and prevent people from living as they want to. For example, governments can influence behaviour by offering higher financial incentives to men than to women for taking child-rearing leaves; or can offer more total paid child-rearing leave if both members of a couple take it than if only one of them does so.

Affirmative action

Rawls draws an important distinction between ideal theory and non-ideal theory. Ideal theory tells us what constitutes justice when there is full compliance by all parties. In non-ideal theory we have to think about what we ought to do when not everyone is in compliance with the demands of justice. The conditions that give rise to the demands for affirmative action (and that underlie the other issues we are considering in this chapter) are, pretty clearly, non-ideal. But Rawls restricts his ambition to developing a theory of justice on ideal assumptions, so it is worth being cautious about the implications of his theory in non-ideal cases. Consider the following argument. Fair equality of opportunity is clearly not in place in the United States: black Americans face worse prospects than whites which are not grounded in their being less talented or less willing to exercise effort. But the measures involved in affirmative action violate the rights of better-qualified whites, which rights are guaranteed by the Liberty Principle. Since the Liberty Principle has priority in Rawls's theory, consistent application of the theory will therefore rule out affirmative action. Ignore the possibility that there may be affirmative action mechanisms which do not violate the Liberty Principle. Even if affirmative action inevitably violated the Liberty principle the argument would not go through, because, in non-ideal conditions like ours, it may be permissible to violate the Liberty Principle for the sake of making society more just. We simply don't know.

So anything I say must be treated with caution. But I don't think that the Liberty Principle does count against many affirmative action mechanisms, because the basic liberties do not include any right to discriminate in employment on the basis of sex or ethnic group membership, and neither do they include anything like the right of the most qualified to be hired, or to be admitted to university. So it seems consistent even with the Liberty Principle, and, even more, Rawls's theory as a whole, that we use affirmative action mechanisms to promote fair equality of opportunity or better to realize the Difference Principle in societies like the United States where race is a central marker of social injustice. But it is also worth noting that affirmative action does not have any special standing according to the theory. It is to be deployed in support of implementing the second principle of justice, but so must many other strategies, including, for example, educational policy measures to benefit children from disadvantaged backgrounds, whether or not they are members of disadvantaged ethnic groups.

The capability approach is rather similar in not giving any special place to affirmative action, or to racial discrimination as a source of unequal opportunity. It is difficult to know how it comments on affirmative action, partly because it is not clear what distributive rule we are supposed to be working with. So, for simplicity's sake, let's suppose that justice requires us to equalize people's capability sets. Now, Sen in particular draws attention to the inequalities of functionings between black and white Americans. He points out that whereas 83 per cent of white American men survive to the age of 75, only 67 per cent of black American men do, and the gap is only slightly less between white and black American women (Sen 1999: 22–3). He also observes that these inequalities are not 'natural' but can be traced to inequalities of wealth, living conditions, healthcare, education provision, and so on. Poverty, in particular, understood relatively to the society in which one lives, seems to be a major source of functioning deprivation and, Sen thinks, capability deprivation. So it might seem that the capabilities approach is very favourable to affirmative action. But that seems wrong. Whether affirmative action is justified depends only on whether it renders more equal the capability sets that people have. Some affirmative action measures will do this, but others will not, and there is no *presumption* in favour of affirmative action. In particular, those forms of affirmative action, such as in admissions to law school and medical school, which tend directly to benefit people who are already among the more advantaged in terms of capabilities are not urgent in the way as, say, providing more resources to primary schooling and healthcare of the poorest children. The capability approach gives priority to the elimination of poverty, whoever suffers it, not to benefiting those who are descended from victims of past injustice.

Both justice as fairness and the capability approach look at the patterns of unequal opportunity and try to resolve them regardless of how the patterns came about. So, if class-based remedies were more efficient ways of overcoming race-tracking inequalities of opportunity than was affirmative action, they would both prefer those remedies. By contrast, Nozick's theory gives a very special place to affirmative action, certainly as it is practised in the United States. Eliminating poverty is not a goal for Nozick; but correcting for past infractions of the principles of justice in acquisition and transfer is. The practices of slavery and, within living memory, the legally enforced segregation practised in the southern states in the United States both constitute straightforward and quite extreme violations of Nozick's principle of justice in transfer. If you assume that many American whites have enjoyed greater inheritances, and many American blacks have enjoyed smaller inheritances, than they would have done absent these violations, you can see how a case for affirmative action, conceived of as a way of correcting, not for poverty, but for those past violations, would emerge. And the objection that many affirmative action programmes benefit people who are already relatively advantaged would have no weight: it does not matter on Nozick's view that the beneficiaries are already well off, just that they are being compensated for an injustice that befell them. This injustice is not slavery, because no beneficiaries of affirmative action today are or were slaves; it is the injustice of receiving less inheritance than would have been predicted had their forebears not been slaves or second-class citizens.

Some opponents of affirmative action point out that contemporary black Americans are not, typically, worse off than they would have been absent the institution of slavery, because, of course, they would not have been born, or if they had been born, they would have been born in Africa, where they would not, clearly, be better off than they are now. The first claim is certainly true, just as it is true that absent the Norman invasion of Britain no-one reading this book can be sure that they would have been born (and I, certainly, would not have been, so would not have written it). But if we reject the justification of affirmative action that appeals to past violations of justice in transfer on these grounds, then we have to reject any kind of recompense for slavery even in the immediately following generation, and even when slavery was an indigenous institution. Imagine that slavery is suddenly adopted in contemporary Britain, and that the Glum family owns slaves for several generations. The Glums coerce their slaves into breeding with each other, over several generations. In the penultimate generation they suddenly free the children, whom they have not used as slaves, and who therefore have no claim to compensation for having been slaves themselves. The children nevertheless demand compensation for having been born to slaves on the ground that the Glums have appropriated the product of their forebears' labour, which is, therefore, not available for them to inherit. The Glums' children can quite rightly say: 'But look, you are not worse off than you would be if our parents hadn't had slaves. *You* owe your very existence to their ownership of slaves. They, indeed, wrongly violated Nozick's principles, and we have benefited from that. But we owe you nothing.' I don't think we would find this a persuasive retort. But the only difference between the Glums' response and that of the opponents of affirmative action that we are considering is in the amount of time that has passed since the wrong.

Equality of opportunity

The priority Rawls grants to fair equality of opportunity and the peculiarly strong way that he understands that demand indicate that his theory, even taken as a whole, condemns inequalities of prospects that have their source solely in material inequalities of family background. But, as I have indicated already, some inequalities in prospects may permissibly have their source in family life, when they arise from activities which are protected by the priority of the Liberty Principle. Exactly what is protected by the value of the family is not clear, though Rawls does provide a suggestive method for thinking about it. He says that the family is part of the Basic Structure in that family members cannot violate the basic freedoms other members have as a matter of membership in a well-ordered society. But, of course, 'we wouldn't want political principles of justice to apply directly to the internal life of the family' (JF 165). So in order to establish exactly what is protected by freedom of association, he says we should follow the general procedure of distinguishing

> between the point of view of people as citizens and their point of view as members of families and of other associations. As citizens we have reasons to impose the constraints specified by the political principles of justice on association; while as members of associations we have reasons for limiting those constraints so that they leave room for a free and flourishing internal life appropriate to the association in question. (JF 165)

This suggests that we should try to work out what kinds of interaction are deeply constitutive of the value of the family, and then say that any measures aimed at promoting equality of opportunity are permissible only if they leave plenty of room in our lives for those sorts of interaction. According to Adam Swift (in press), this strategy supports the idea that the Liberty Principle protects intimate interactions which may, as a side-effect, enhance a child's competitive advantage, but it does not protect gifting or leaving large amounts of money to our children, or being able to spend money on providing them with expensive elite private schooling. The details may be disputable, of course, but the strategy is clear.

Even this strategy, though, assumes that the priority of the Liberty Principle is a constraint in non-ideal theory. But there is no reason to suppose that Rawls thinks this: so it may be permissible to be more intrusive than even Swift would allow to secure equality of opportunity. However, there is an important difference between the problems to which affirmative action is offered as a solution and the problem of equality of opportunity and the family. The problems to which affirmative action is a proposed solution are past violations of liberal justice; the problem goes away in ideal theory. But the problem that the family affects people's life prospects does not go away in ideal theory; even in a perfectly just society we can expect these mechanisms to operate, and so ideal theory has to have something to say about them.

Just as it gives no special standing to the victims of past infractions of justice, the capability approach is not concerned with the particular sources of inequalities of capabilities. It sees the family as valuable in so far as it is a source of flourishing for the people involved in it, and understands that many of the resources needed for developing one's capabilities are provided within the family. But it does not see, for example, the ability to confer one's wealth on one's children, or to use it to provide them with opportunities superior to those others will have, as essential to the family's ability to develop adequately the capabilities of the children or to realize the flourishing of the adults. So, like justice as fairness, it gives the family a special place, but, again like justice as fairness, it objects to the family's tendency to promote inequalities of opportunity and seeks ways to mitigate the inegalitarian effects of family arrangements without undermining the ability of those arrangements to bring flourishing to participants.

Nozick is very explicit, and not surprisingly, in his rejection of any ideal of equal opportunity. The central problem with equality of opportunity is that the means to it would intrinsically involve violating people's basic rights:

> There are two ways to attempt to provide such equality: by directly worsening the situations of those more favored with the opportunity, or by improving the situations of those less well-favored. The latter requires the use of resources, and so it too involves worsening the situation of some: those from whom the holdings are taken in order to improve the situation of others. But holdings to which those people are entitled may not be seized, even to provide equality of opportunity for others. (Nozick 1974: 235)

If someone enjoys a greater share of the world's resources, to which she is entitled under the entitlement theory, she is also entitled to dispose of them as she will; and if this means that her children will enjoy more opportunity than other people's children, justice protects that kind of intergenerational transmission of advantage. It doesn't require it: she might, if she wants, gift or will her holdings to children who have worse prospects than her own; her children have no claim or entitlement to the resources independently of her desire to transfer them. But equality of opportunity simply has no place in the theory. Nozick's rejection of equality of opportunity emphasizes a particular feature of his theory. On, for example, Rawls's theory, there are principles – the Liberty Principle, fair equality of opportunity, the Difference Principle – which sometimes conflict. From the fact that they conflict, we cannot conclude that we should reject any of them. We simply look for reasons to prioritize one over the other when conflicts arise. Absent conflict, we apply the subordinate principle. But this is possible because the Liberty Principle, for example, only makes limited comment on what should be done: it requires that certain liberties be preserved, but this is consistent with a wide range of rules about the distribution of opportunities and income. Nozick's entitlement theory is totalizing. Although it is consistent with a wide range of income and opportunity distributions, it is consistent with only one rule regarding their distribution, the rule that it, itself, specifies: that they must be distributed as is dictated by the choices of the legitimate owners of holdings. So there is no room for any subordinate principles of justice: when we find a conflict we have to reject the conflicting principle.

Whereas Nozick is hostile to the very idea of equality of opportunity, the group-rights theorists are not. However, the group rights that Halbertal and Margalit endorse, and those that Kymlicka entertains, are liable to work against equality of opportunity, especially equality of opportunity between the children coming from minority groups and those from the majority group. Consider language rights. Suppose that the Welsh have a right to impose Welsh-language-only instruction in all their schools, and to conduct all official business in Welsh, and that a result is the emergence of a small number of monolingual Welsh speakers. Relative to English speakers, as I argued above, this group would have unequal opportunity for many important goods: job opportunities, opportunities to read great literature, a pool of potential marital partners, and so on. This is a case of inequality of opportunity tracking a particular kind of family circumstance, of course: the idea is that whatever the prospects of the monolingual Welsh speaker, the prospects of the otherwise equally disadvantaged English speaker are superior. There could be no inequality of opportunity (based in the family) *within* each community, and one would still expect inequality of opportunity across them. The cultural liberal theories take no stand on the intergenerational transmission of advantage, but the rights they propose are liable to produce inequalities across a particular dimension.

The gendered division of labour

Does Rawls's theory also condemn the gendered division of labour and the inequality between the sexes that it manifests and engenders? Some feminist commentators think so. Susan Moller Okin, in particular, argues that, properly reformulated, justice as fairness impugns the gender system. She takes fair equality of opportunity to mean that 'if any roles or positions analogous to our current sex roles, including those of husband and wife, mother and father, were to survive the demands of the [Difference Principle], [fair equality of opportunity] would disallow any linkage between these roles and sex' (Okin 1987: 66–7). She goes on to invoke three particular aspects of Rawls's theory which illustrate its inconsistency with the gender system. First, the Liberty Principle protects, as one of the basic liberties, the important liberty of free choice of occupation: 'It is not difficult to see that this liberty is compromised by the assumption and customary expectation, central to our gender system, that women take far greater responsibility than men for housework and child care, whether or not they work for wages outside the home' (Okin 1987: 67). Second, Okin thinks, the fair value of the political liberties demands 'equal political representation of men and women [which] especially if they are parents, is clearly inconsistent with our gender system' (Okin 1987: 68).

Finally, Rawls says that the parties in the Original Position ' "would wish to avoid at almost any cost the social conditions that undermine self-respect" which is "perhaps the most important" of all the primary goods' (Okin 1987: 68). So,

> if those in the original position did not know whether they were to be men or women they would surely be concerned to establish a thoroughgoing social and economic equality between the sexes that would preserve either from the need to servilely pander to the prejudices of the other . . . in general they would be unlikely to tolerate basic social institutions that asymmetrically either forced or gave strong incentives to members of one sex to become sex objects for the other. (Okin 1987: 88)

I think Okin is too generous to Rawls. It is true that the theory condemns inequalities of opportunity where those are directly caused by the design of coercive institutions. So not only does the theory prohibit discrimination against women in hiring and access to educational goods, it also impugns the wage-differentials that women face in most economies. There is no basic liberty to discriminate against women in hiring or to pay them less than equally capable men. So the gendered division of labour in the workplace, *in so far as it arises from discrimination* of various kinds, is condemned. But, *in so far as it arises from the choices men and women make* about how to organize their domestic arrangements, Rawls's theory does not object to it, even if those choices are influenced by 'assumption and customary expectation'. Why is this? Because, at least on the most natural reading of what Rawls means by the Basic Structure, a sexist cultural atmosphere is not part of the Basic Structure, because it is not among the major coercive institutions and, officially, it is only those to which the principles of justice apply.

So, to take Okin's particular arguments, the liberty for free choice of occupation means that men and women must both have formally available to them the full array of occupations in the sense that they cannot be discriminated against or unequally rewarded. But if patterns emerge of women choosing not to take certain kinds of jobs, or to be less active in the workforce, or to have jobs which are more flexible but from which promotion is more difficult, that does not show that the liberty has been violated, or unequally provided. Maybe it would be different if Rawls granted fair value to all the liberties, but he doesn't and has good reasons for not doing so.

Rawls does grant fair value to the political liberties, but this does not, in fact, require equal representation of men and women. What it requires is that each individual has available to them equal resources for political engagement, regardless of other inequalities between them. But it is consistent with this that some groups of people systematically put less energy into political engagement than others, because they are less interested, or have less time because of other, competing, personal commitments. Men must not accumulate power in a way that makes it impossible for women to engage on an equal basis with them, but if they have power at any given time because women are less engaged, this is not condemned by the fair value of the political liberties.

The observant reader will notice that I have talked very little about the interest in self-respect and its social bases, which Okin invokes as her third aspect of the theory. This is because, although Okin is right that Rawls says that self-respect is a vitally important primary good, he says very little about what that means in practice, independently of the principles of justice. I'm pretty confident that Okin is right to say that concern for the social bases of self-respect would impugn not only the formal structures of sex discrimination but also the cultural assumptions about gender that influence our choices. But I am not confident about invoking this in Rawls's defence. The main reason is this: the theory itself consists only of the principles of justice as they apply to the Basic Structure. The idea of self-respect and its social basis is sufficiently vague that if it is brought in independently of the theory of justice itself, it can support many different and conflicting perfectionist measures. Some might say that ungodliness, or unfriendliness, or lack of community, inhibits our sense of self-respect, and they might say so for good reason. Does this mean that we should impugn those aspects of our culture which support those phenomena? I don't think that Rawls would want to say so, and so I think he should resist Okin's arguments.

I should be clear here that although I have *formally* been criticizing Okin, I see my comments as really supporting criticism of Rawls. I think Okin is right to see the gender system as a source of injustice against women (though also one that makes many men worse off in the ways that really matter than they would be without it). In chapter 8 I shall explore a way of reinterpreting Rawls's account of the Basic Structure that would allow him to respond more favourably to Okin; in fact it is the interpretation that I suspect she has in mind. But for the moment at least I emphasize that his theory is less amenable to feminist aims than he might want.

One of the prominent defenders of the capability approach, Martha Nussbaum, is herself a renowned feminist theorist, who has deployed this approach to feminist theoretical ends. What is striking is that the approach appears to comment not only on those restrictions the approach on people's capabilities that are directly imposed by law, but also on those that are shaped by customs and social norms. So whereas Rawls's theory objects to the gendered division of labour when it is maintained by legal restrictions and economic incentives, the capability approach objects to it however it is maintained. Even if women are legally permitted to work outside the home at the same jobs as men, and have access to equal educational resources to help them attain the same level of qualification, if their uptake of those opportunities and positions is lower because they are inhibited by having internalized social norms, that is, *prima facie*, objectionable.

Does this judgement depend on the idea that the work to which women are assigned in the gendered division of labour is somehow less important or rewarding than that to which men are assigned? I don't think so. Whereas some tasks in the 'female' sphere seem intrinsically unrewarding (keeping the doorstep clean), most are not, and some – especially child-rearing – are not only profoundly challenging and rewarding, but also intrinsically valuable. Similarly, many of the activities in the 'male' sphere, while possibly interesting, are not obviously worthwhile (refraining from making obviously justified criticisms of one's superiors). But there is no need to deny this in order to condemn the gendered nature of the division of labour. Some women may be much better suited to activities in the 'male' sphere than to those in the female sphere, and vice versa, so that those people do not have as many opportunities as others for flourishing if they are restricted to their own sphere. Some women may be stifled by a life of child-rearing and domestic labour, however intrinsically valuable it is; some men may be frustrated by a life of 'breadwinning', however interesting many others may find it. The norms which present barriers to their finding lives in which they can flourish are, for that reason, condemned by the capability approach.

As you might expect, Nozick's theory is broadly unsympathetic to criticism of the gendered division of labour *per se*. Of course, his view does not assign different roles to men and women, and a consequence of his theory is that men and women should not be legally assigned (or encouraged to take on) different roles in the workforce or in the home. But it is also adamant that those who own firms are entitled to hire whomever they will to work for them, and to transact with whomever they want as customers. If prevailing social norms lead owners of companies to discriminate against women in hiring, that is something they have a right to do, and it would be wrong for the government coercively to interfere. Similarly, if a patterned division of labour within the household emerges as the result of negotiations between persons who share domiciles, that is their business, and it would be wrong of the government to try to influence them otherwise, even if their behaviour was influenced by background social norms. It is worth noting that social norms could come to have a magnified effect on the gendered nature of the division of labour if, as Nozick says, employers must be free to discriminate against women. If employers take up that permission, and do discriminate against women, this will mean women have far fewer opportunities than men outside the home. This, in turn, will impact their negotiating power within the home: they cannot bring in as much money as their husbands from outside the home, so they have less bargaining power when it comes to deciding who will do the lion's share of domestic labour. If you don't like the idea that couples (or, as in Nozick's world, triples, quadruples or however many people constitute a household) *bargain* over who does what, think of the couple instead as a rational united agent, trying to decide how to maximize its well-being. Since the man, other things being equal, can derive more income than the woman from working outside the home, the couple have an incentive to assign domestic labour to the woman, while the man works outside the home. Even if they both work outside the home, it is rational for them to put his career first – she is the one who should stay off work when the kids are sick, or take time off to look after an ailing relative, or take a part-time job in order to be able to manage the household and care for the children after school. The social norms work twice: first, by influencing how the couple want to do things within the home; second, by allowing massive restrictions on what women can do outside the home. But if the norms were different, and had different consequences, Nozick would not have a basis for objecting to those either. Unlike, perhaps, some conservative thinkers who believe that the specific gendered division of labour we know serves some good purpose, and should be reinforced for that reason, Nozick is indifferent to it.

What, finally, of the group-rights approach? Just as I suspect this approach will tend to reinforce mechanisms producing inequality of opportunity, there's a good case that, depending on what specific group rights are admitted, it will reinforce, rather than work against, the gendered division of labour. In a well-known essay called 'Is Multiculturalism Bad for Women?' Susan Moller Okin argues that all cultures are to some degree sexist: that is, hostile to the interests of women (conceived as equal to men). Okin worries that there are many formal, and informal, ways of restricting women's freedom and access to resources. Here are three of her more telling examples:

1   Marriage by capture is practised in the Hmong community in the United States. Marriages are arranged by the parents of women (as young as 14), and the selected future husband 'kidnaps' the bride-to-be (with the consent of her parents) and rapes her, then marries her. Sometimes the young woman has been consulted concerning what will happen, and sometimes she has not, and of course the moral quality of the practice is somewhat affected by whether or not there has been consultation; but for any children below the age of consent, even

consultation mitigates the wrong done to them only very slightly (Okin 1999: 18).

2   On some understandings of Islamic law, adultery, when committed by a woman, is punishable by death, the sentence to be carried out by male blood relatives of the adulteress (Okin 1999: 18).

3   While the previous two examples are straightforwardly outlawed by most Western democracies, and straightforwardly contradict the interests which both Kymlicka and Halbertal and Margalit advance in support of group-based rights, Okin's third case is more complicated. Female genital mutilation practices vary, but the main practices are the removal of the clitoris (clitoridectomy) and the stitching together of the two sides of the vulva, leaving a tiny opening for urination and menstruation (infibulation). In the most extreme form genital mutilation also involves the removal of the whole of the labia minora and the labia majora. The practice brings no medical benefit, and carries with it great risks, including, but not limited to, risks of haemorrhage, infection, urine retention, chronic pelvic infection, infertility, urinary tract infection, perineal lacerations and puerperal sepsis. The operation is also extremely painful. Figures are not available for the extent of this practice in the West, though it is thought to be fairly widespread among African immigrants. The World Health Organization estimates that 137 million women in African countries have suffered this form of mutilation, including some 93 per cent of women in Mali, 89 per cent in the Sudan and 98 per cent in Somalia (Okin 1999: 18).[1]

While standard liberal individualist views will have no problem prohibiting female genital mutilation, group-rights versions will have more difficulty. While individualists typically allow parents considerable latitude over the raising of their children, they will normally say that parents are not permitted to impose on their children substantial risks of great physical harm when there is no reasonable prospect of there being a correlative benefit (for the child). But the group-rights view allows that the group may impose costs (or set up a system which results in costs being imposed) on an individual for the sake of the survival of the cultural structure that is in place. Halbertal and Margalit, as we have seen, do not make a distinction between the culture of parent and child, and so it may be that, if female genital mutilation is a practice deeply engrained in the culture the group rights are supposed to protect, it must be permitted.

In fact I doubt that self-declaredly liberal group-rights theorists will usually want to endorse permitting the practice of female genital mutilation. But Okin makes a further, and perhaps more telling, point. She says that 'sex discrimination is often far less overt. In many cultures strict control of women is enforced in the private sphere by the authority of actual or symbolic fathers often acting through, or with the complicity of, the older women of the culture' (Okin 1999: 22). Think, for example, of upbringing into traditional sex roles, into traditional attitudes of subordination to men, of differential attitudes to education. Many of these practices do not require that women be formally denied equal rights or equal resources, and allow for women to have equal standing before the law. But the practices gently shape the attitudes of men and women so that women end up having fewer informal opportunities, and claiming fewer resources than men. In particular, girls and boys can be reared to take up their differential places in the status order without any formal interference form the state or the authorities to ensure that this is so. So the liberal culturalist theories, even when, as in Kymlicka's case, they seem to be opposed to sexist legal restrictions, protect from scrutiny those sexist practices that survive not through the enforcement of legal restriction but through the observance of cultural norms.

Okin's point has two dimensions. First, she notes that cultures cannot be presumed to be good for the people who live in them, and that because of the pervasiveness of sex discrimination, for the vast majority of cultures (in fact, probably all cultures), being granted group rights will entail that they are able to impose internal restrictions (whether formal or informal) on some of their members. Second, she fears that group protections, even if they do not formally allow more powerful members of the group to oppress the others, will have the effect (unintended by their defenders) of validating the problematic practices within the culture, and rendering those practices more resistant to criticism both from without and from within. To illustrate the latter possibility, consider the familiar practice of conservatives in liberal democracies of responding to arguments for reform that they are unpatriotic, or 'not the way we do things here'. Conservatives within minority groups can make the same move against internal reformers, and more successfully when there is some public validation of 'the way we do things here'.

Kymlicka, at least, might respond to the first point by counting socialization into traditional sex roles, and other similar informal practices, as 'internal restrictions' which cannot be defended from a liberal group-rights perspective. But this raises the question of what counts as an internal restriction. Certainly, within mainstream liberal societies we do not think it appropriate for the state to prohibit parents from socializing their children into traditional sex roles, even if we might think (as Okin does) that it is legitimate for the state to act in ways that make it less likely that people will do so. It is hard to believe that something which could not legitimately be forbidden in a standard individual rights regime can count as an internal restriction within a protected group. Okin is not arguing that such practices should be outlawed either within the group or within the mainstream society. She is arguing that group-based protections make such objectionable (but not necessarily prohibitable) practices more likely to persist within the groups, and that this is a cost which *members of the group* will have to bear which must be taken into account when deciding whether to grant group-based protections.

Conclusion

I've tried to illustrate the practical consequences of the theories for these particular issues, for two purposes. The first is to illustrate and engage somewhat in the method of reflective equilibrium that I presented in chapter 2: the consequences of the theories for actual cases might affect our judgements about the theories themselves. So, for example, I often find that people who are well disposed to Rawls's theory when they encounter the arguments for the principles and the principles themselves are discomforted by the observation that the theory gives no in-principle support to affirmative action; and also that some people deeply committed to affirmative action as a matter of principle warm somewhat to Nozick's theory when they see that its reasoning about affirmative action closely matches their own. Of course, this does not mean that the intuition about the case should always be decisive: sometimes you should reject that intuition, especially if, say, you find that with respect to a wide range of other cases the theory in question goes against your intuitions. The second purpose has been to illustrate the slippage between theory and practice: it is very difficult to know for any given theory exactly what it would say about any particular situation or case.

8
Personal Justice, Political Justice and Liberal Feminism

Throughout this book I have followed what I take to be the mainstream view in contemporary political philosophy, which is that the Basic Structure of society is the main subject of justice. Justice, in other words, is about finding the principles which guide the design of the coercive or, to use the term in its broadest sense, political institutions, rather than about finding the principles which should guide individuals' behaviour. Rawls coins the phrase 'the Basic Structure as subject', but most of the other theorists we have looked at, from the libertarians to the egalitarians to the theorists of group rights, accept this basic ground rule. In the previous chapter we saw that this view makes it difficult for liberals to claim, as they might want to, that certain kinds of inequality of opportunity which arise from within the family are unjust.

In this chapter I want to look at a criticism of this assumption, the modern version of which originates in the feminist movement, but which has much older roots. The objection is encapsulated in the famous slogan 'the personal is political' and says that there is no reason for a theory of justice to restrict its attention to the Basic Structure – the personal behaviour of individuals is just as much a matter for evaluation against the criterion of justice as is the coercive activity of public authorities.

This objection should not be confused with a different objection which says, to Rawls, or perhaps more commonly to libertarians, that they fail to recognize the public nature of some institutions, and so mischaracterize the Basic Structure. The mischaracterization objection acknowledges a distinction between the public and private spheres, but asserts that more is properly included in the public than is usually recognized. So libertarians tend to treat the activities of capitalist corporations as if they are non-coercive and therefore not open to criticism from the perspective of justice. Some theorists treat the family the same way, and Rawls himself over time vacillated between including the family in the Basic Structure and excluding it: treating it, in effect, as private.

The 'personal is political' objection says that individuals' behaviours and motivations are themselves subjects of evaluation from the perspective of justice, in so far as they are responses to the informal prevailing cultural expectations or social norms. Recall my response to Susan Moller Okin's argument that Rawls's theory of justice would impugn the gendered division of labour. She characterized the gender system as consisting not only in the laws of a society and the incentives built into its economic system, but also in the prevailing norms and expectations which influence individual choices to align sex with gender. I responded that in so far as the gender system is partly constituted by those norms, Rawls's theory does not impugn it, because in his theory the principles do not apply to the latter, only to laws and economic incentives. The 'personal is political' objection says that, if so, Rawls's theory is wrong (and so are those like Nozick's, Kymlicka's, and perhaps Nussbaum and Sen's, that follow that line). The political philosopher who has pressed this objection most forcefully in recent years is G.A. Cohen, so it is on his argument that I shall concentrate, before moving on to discuss the implications of this view for feminism.

Cohen's argument focuses on Rawls, and in particular argues that the Difference Principle (maximin) cannot just apply to the social institutions, but must also apply to the individual choices of agents. But it does so because Rawls articulates reasons for a view that many others just take for granted, and because Cohen is especially concerned to undermine the Difference Principle. So although I shall present it as an argument against Rawls, it is in fact an argument against a view shared almost across the political spectrum of theorists of justice.

Cohen's argument is rather complicated, but I want to represent it properly before making any comment on it. Here it is in full.

The argument starts with an observation about the kind of justification someone who benefited from permitted inequalities would have to give for their accepting these benefits. The Difference Principle says that inequalities are just if and only if they are necessary to make the worst off people in society better off than they would otherwise be (Cohen 1997: 5). This principle mechanism supports inequalities when incentives for the talented can benefit the least advantaged, by inducing the talented to work more productively: 'talented people will produce more than they otherwise would if and only if they are paid more than an ordinary wage, and some of the extra . . . can be recruited on behalf of the worst off' (Cohen 1997: 6). Think about the talented recipients of the incentives. Either they themselves affirm the Difference Principle or they do not. Suppose that they do not: then the society is not just in the appropriate Rawlsian sense for a society is fully just if and only if its member themselves affirm and uphold the correct principles of justice (Rawls stipulates this as part of the idea of a well-ordered society).

Let's suppose, instead, that the talented people themselves *do* endorse the Difference Principle. If they do, then they apply the principles in their daily life. But then they are unable to answer the question: why do you require more pay than the untalented get for work that is not especially unpleasant?

> They cannot claim in *self-justification* at the bar of the difference principle that their high rewards are necessary through their own unwillingness to work for ordinary rewards as productively as they do for exceptionally high ones, an unwillingness which ensures that the untalented get less than they otherwise would. . . . [So] the justice of a society is not exclusively a function of its legislative structure . . . but also of the choices people make within those rules. (Cohen 1997: 9)

Defenders of the mainstream view have a response to this kind of awkwardness. They say that the Difference Principle applies only to the Basic Structure of society, because justice is only a matter of the design of the Basic Structure. People do not need to offer self-justification, and they do not need to think about the choices in the light of the principles of justice, as long as they obey the laws and maintain the social structures required by those principles. This is what Cohen calls the Basic Structure objection, and it constitutes the view we are discussing. But, Cohen responds, Rawls says two things that contradict the Basic Structure objection. First, Rawls says that the least advantaged can 'bear their position with dignity' because they know they are better off than the least advantaged would be under any other distribution; no improvement in that position is possible. But Cohen points out that it is false that no improvement is possible, because even within a Basic Structure which is set up to the maximal benefit of the least advantaged, the least advantaged would be better off if the more advantaged refused the benefits of the inequality. They *could* work harder without the incentives; but they *wouldn't*. And the least advantaged, at least if they have a basic understanding of economics, know this. So it is not true that the mere satisfaction of the Difference Principle at the level of the Basic Structure enables the least advantaged to 'bear their position with dignity'.

Second, Rawls says that people act *from* the principles of justice in their daily lives. But this suggests that justice is partly a function of individual choices: if the Basic Structure objection were correct, then there would be no need for them to act from the principles.

Now, of course, Rawls says a lot of things, and over a long career it is reasonable for someone to contradict himself once or twice. Maybe, then, he shouldn't have made the comments which contradict the Basic Structure objection. So Cohen recognizes that he has to make a more positive argument against this objection. He points out that Rawls is systematically ambiguous between two accounts of what the Basic Structure is. Cohen calls the two accounts the *Broad Coercive Outline* account and the *Major Social Institutions* account. The Broad Coercive Outline account says that what are included in the Basic Structure are only those institutions which are (legally) coercive (Cohen 1997: 19). The Major Social Institutions account is much broader and includes the rules and conventions of accepted practice (Cohen 1997: 19–20). To see the distinction, think of the Amish, a religious community in parts of the American East Coast and Midwest. Amish children are subject to almost the same laws as non-Amish children (the exception is that they are allowed to stop attending school at an earlier age). Once they reach the age of majority they cannot be required to attend religious services, or remain within the community, and in fact Amish culture allows for a period of time in late adolescence when children are expected to flout the rules of their society before they choose whether to remain in it or leave it. However, the cost of exit is that they will be shunned henceforth by their community, including their families, and they know this. This practice is not coercive, in a formal sense – the law does nothing to uphold or prohibit it. But it nevertheless counts as a major social institution (in their micro-society).

But the non-coercive institutions only have the character they do because of the choices that people routinely make within the coercive institutions. On the Broad Social Institutions account, then, personal behaviour and personal choices are part of the Basic Structure, and themselves subject to evaluation from the perspective of justice. So the only way of resisting Cohen's argument is by holding to the Broad Coercive Outline account.

However, the Broad Coercive Outline account flies in the face of the reasons that Rawls gives for focusing on the Basic Structure. He says that the reason for caring about the Basic Structure is that 'its effects are so profound and present from the start' (Cohen 1997: 21), and that 'since any modern society . . . must rely on some inequalities to be well designed and effectively organised' we look at the Basic Structure because of its 'profound and pervasive influence on the persons who live under its institutions' (JF 55). This is the only way of explaining the primacy of the Basic Structure. But, Cohen points out, it is false that the effects of only the coercive institutions are profound and present from the start, and Rawls himself seems to be aware of this. The two obvious examples of non-coercive institutions whose effects are profound and present from birth are the family structure, and the way that people respond to the incentive structure of the economy.

Think about the family structure. If a society has a sexist ethos, so that both men and women generally regard women as primarily responsible for domestic labour, then supposing that both men and women are expected to work outside the home, women will end up carrying an unequal burden – working the same amount outside, but more inside, the home. This practice will, in turn, predictably influence the children being brought up by those parents, and their own expectations concerning how to live their own lives. No law, or coercive apparatus surrounding the law, is needed to maintain such an arrangement, so it will not show up as institutional on the Broad Coercive Outline account. But it is clearly an inequality that is 'profound and present from the start'. And, for Cohen, it seems obvious that a society in which domestic labour is unequally shared between men and women is, in that respect, less just than one in which it is equally shared, even if the reason that it is unequally shared is unrelated to the coercive background.

Think now about individual responses to the incentive structure in the economy. The incentive structure suggested by the Difference Principle aims to get talented people who otherwise would not exercise their talents to do so in order that the state can redistribute the surplus their work generates to the least advantaged, thus improving the latter's position. Obviously the state cannot impose a marginal tax rate of 100 per cent, because it would then be providing no incentive. So it must impose a tax rate of less than 100 per cent. So consider two different societies, A and B, in which the tax rates (and therefore the broad coercive outlines) are identical. In A, talented individuals are highly concerned with the interests of the least advantaged: they are willing to work at much lower salaries in positions that directly advantage the least advantaged. In B, talented individuals are highly self-interested: they are willing to work only at very high salaries, so that despite the identical marginal tax rates, they end up taking home much more income.

There are two possible scenarios. In one, the least advantaged have a lower net real income in B than in A; in the other they have the same net real income as in A, but they know that if only the talented individuals were motivated the way talented individuals are motivated in A, they (the least advantaged) would have a much higher net real income. Either way, the motivations of the talented, and not the coercive institutions, cause them to be worse off than they otherwise would be.

Cohen admits the difficulty of knowing how to assign blame for the resultant injustices, but this is not important: we can say that one state of affairs is more just than another without knowing how blame should be distributed for the wrongs in the less just state of affairs. The key point that I want to highlight about Cohen's analysis is that when comparing how just two societies are it is appropriate to take into account not only those features of people's situations that arise from the directly coercive institutions, but also those that arise, indirectly, from the customs, culture and ethos of a society, even when those are not enforced coercively. A society with a more equal distribution of wealth is more just than one with a less equal distribution of wealth even when they have identically maximining coercive structures, if the only difference is that the ethos of the less equal society encourages people to behave in a maximizing way.

If Cohen is right, then justice comments on a great deal more than has been admitted by most of the theorists we have encountered so far. On Cohen's preferred understanding of the Basic Structure, Rawls's theory can indeed be put to the use Okin seeks, and impugns the gender system, as well as the inequalities that Cohen thinks are unjust because they are made necessary by the self-seeking motivations of talented individuals. What already seemed a radical theory becomes an even more radical theory: radically egalitarian and radically feminist.

Is the personal political in the way that Cohen suggests? I want to mention briefly three responses to Cohen's argument, and then look, again briefly, at a final theory of justice, which tries to reconfigure the relationship between the personal and the political.

The first response would be to concede everything that Cohen says, but then comment that it makes no practical difference. One might observe that we simply have no idea how to ensure that the culture has the right kind of content. Cohen provides the nice example of British businessmen in the 1950s meeting their American counterparts and, because they come from a more egalitarian culture, being shocked by, rather than envious of, the much greater inequality between the Americans and their employees than the British enjoy. But how did the British culture of the 1950s get to be that way? Even if we knew for sure, we would not know how to replicate the influences through government action. The public culture of the United States has become somewhat more tolerant of homosexuality since the 1970s (even fierce opponents of homosexuality now feel obliged to proclaim that they 'love the sinner, but hate the sin', and most probably do so more or less sincerely), and much less racist, and no doubt government action has had some impact; but for the most part the change has come about as a result of processes that the government neither set in motion nor had much control over.

This is a good reason for, in practice, refraining from intervening in the character and development of a culture. But not for refusing to license government action when it might be effective. So think now about what it would take for the government to succeed in controlling the 'patterns of interpretation and evaluation' that manifest themselves in individuals' judgements and choices about how to live. The most natural means available are the education of children, and the public education of adults. It would have to use its control over the means of public education to alter the patterns of interpretation and evaluation. It is hard to see how it could do this without promoting particular attitudes to homosexuality, for example, or toward different religious and anti-religious views. That is, it would have to involve itself in shaping the minds of prospective adults.

It is worth remembering at this point that governments typically do use their control over schooling in this manner, in both obvious and less obvious ways. Governments frequently use schooling to inculcate patriotic sentiment in children, or to promote some sort of religious faith. Public schools in democratic countries often also promote democratic character in various ways: they encourage children to vote, to value public service, to think critically about public matters, to be tolerant of those they disagree with, and so on.

Less obviously, by prioritizing some curriculum subjects over others they foster the kinds of character that studying those subjects tends to produce. So while it may sound authoritarian to shape character through schooling, it is not unusual.

The second response to Cohen is developed by Andrew Williams. Williams acknowledges that there is no principled reason to define the subject of justice simply as the legally coercive structure. But he thinks that Cohen moves too fast in assuming that the Basic Structure can be defined only in terms of either its coercive nature or its tendency to influence people's lives profoundly. An alternative definition can be developed by reference to the emphasis Rawls places on the value of publicity. Rawls says, 'By an institution I shall understand a *public system of rules*' (Williams 1998: 233). He reserves the term 'institutional' for activity that realizes a certain type of norm which is public in the following sense: individuals are able to attain common knowledge of (i) the rules' general applicability, (ii) their particular requirements and (iii) the extent to which individuals conform with those requirements. So Rawlsian principles demand

> the establishment and maintenance of those institutions that are most effective in achieving such goals and they condemn institutions that frustrate their achievement. However those principles are inapplicable to certain types of decision. For some choices, although they may be profoundly influential, cannot be regarded as according with or violating public rules ... moreover, amongst such non-institutional choices is the decision to become a market-maximizer rather than extend egalitarian conviction to one's economic activity. (Williams 1998: 234)

On this account Rawls's theory of justice, and the choice to apply it to a public system of rules, incorporates not only the value of treating individuals as free and equal citizens, but also a particular conception of social unity – the idea that people should live together by rules that they can all accept, which they can all abide by as long as others abide by them, and which they can all know are being followed. On this view different sources of inequality can be treated asymmetrically. Because we can gather information about what the fiscal policy is and the extent to which it is genuinely being implemented, it is a proper object of concern from the point of justice. But individual motivations, about which even the individual involved often has less than perfect information, cannot be publicly monitored. On this conception of the purpose of a theory of justice the *fact of limited information* bears on the evaluation of competing theories of justice. We should select principles 'whose scope is restricted to publicly accessible phenomena', because our major reason for caring about such sources of inequality is 'not simply their differential impact on people's lives' but also their public nature (Williams 1998: 245).

Similarly, consider the gendered division of labour. We can, indeed, monitor whether laws and economic incentives are designed in a way that systematically disadvantages women; and in so far as they do, it is appropriate to say that the society is unjust. But suppose that we can observe that women systematically do more of certain kinds of domestic labour despite our having long ago successfully eliminated legal restrictions and economic incentives which would lead us to expect that outcome. We cannot know whether they are doing so as a result of systematic pressures in the culture, or as a result of natural inclination, or simply as a result of free autonomous choices. We cannot account for the ethos and its character in the way that publicity requires. So the principles of justice should refrain from comment.

Williams's response to Cohen reinstates the limited scope of justice. It says, effectively, that the personal is not political, because the personal is not capable of being publicly monitored. The more equal society is no more just than the less equal society when inequality is produced by the ethos alone. But another possible response would be to concede Cohen's argument, and grant that justice has the wide scope he suggests, but invoke a different value, legitimacy, and say that that value sets constraints on what the state may do to promote justice. The value of legitimacy in fact underlies Rawls's attempt to generate a 'political' liberal theory of justice, one that would be justifiable within a wide range of conceptions of the good life.

What does legitimacy require? I'm going to outline briefly some features which most contemporary accounts of legitimacy share, and explain why these features might make it difficult for the state to pursue justice (legitimately) by trying to manipulate the ethos. On the standard views legitimacy requires first that the government be susceptible to consent of all reasonable persons. But this is a relatively weak demand, because, of course, a government could fulfil this condition without having the consent of any actual persons, even though some of the actual persons are reasonable. To say that reasonable people could consent is not to say that they do or will. So most accounts supplement this with the demand that the government has the actual consent of many actual persons. If you like, the vastly unpopular government that contents itself with the thought that its population *could* consent is simply not trying hard enough. But now we get to the third, and for our purposes most important, condition: *actual consent does not contribute to the legitimacy of a regime if that regime itself has manufactured the consent.* So, for example, suppose that the actual consent were produced by a government department placing a consent-producing drug in the water supply. We would not think that such consent counted, at all, in evaluating whether the regime was legitimate. For consent to count, it has to be the result of the free and unmanipulated reasoning of the citizens themselves. When the government tries to condition the consent, it thereby compromises the legitimacy it would otherwise earn.

This suggests what might be wrong with directing efforts to manipulating the ethos of a society. While it is entirely legitimate for a government to reform the coercive institutions (within the limits set by something like the Liberty Principle) to alter the incentives people face and to alter the share of the total resources they enjoy, direct intervention to alter the character of the ethos runs the risk of being illegitimate. The government should not attempt to reach into and alter the motivational structure of the citizen without directly engaging his or her reason.

Of course, this conception of legitimacy calls into question some of the practices I said earlier are commonplace. On the conception of legitimacy I have outlined, such practices as using public education to promote patriotism, or even loyalty to civic institutions, can be problematic. This could seem like an overwhelming objection if we thought of the relationship between justice and legitimacy in a particular way: if we thought, as Rawls often seems to, that nothing may ever be done to secure justice that violates the principle of legitimacy. But if, instead, we see the two values as competing so that some gains in justice may justify some losses in legitimacy, then we can say that these practices may, sometimes, be justified, but only if they bring a great gain in justice, without sacrificing much in legitimacy.

This response to Cohen allows us to have the best of both worlds. We can say that a more equal state is more *just* than a less equal state, but still say that it may not be permissible, or at least that it may not be, all things considered, better, because the government is limited in what it may permissibly do to promote justice. But it may be more just and equally legitimate; it all depends on the proper explanation of the content of the prevailing ethos. In Cohen's example the distribution of resources between British managers and workers in the 1950s was more just, and no less legitimate, than between American managers and workers, because the postwar ethos in Britain had not arisen through government manipulation of the ethos. But it does not follow that the United States had a legitimate and more just option available; it may well be that it could only have moved toward the more just arrangement through illegitimate manipulation of the ethos.

Feminism, redistribution and recognition

What are the implications of the idea that the Basic Structure should be construed in the broader way that Cohen suggests for feminism, the political stance from which the modern use of the slogan 'the personal is political' originates? Recall again that in chapter 7 I criticized Okin's argument that Rawls's theory of justice condemns the gendered division of labour within the economy and the home. My argument there was that because the principles of justice apply to the Basic Structure of society, which I interpreted as the 'broad coercive outlines' of society, they were insensitive to those aspects of the gendered division of labour that arise from people's individual decisions, where those decisions are responsive to sexist norms in society, rather than to sexist laws, or sexist incentives in the economy. Since some of the gendered division of labour is, according to Okin, constructed by sexist norms, that part cannot be condemned by Rawls's theory.

However, Cohen's reinterpretation of the Basic Structure, in terms of dispositional properties, allows a different response. If we can apply Rawls's principles to the ethos, or culture, as well as to the broad coercive outlines, then, indeed, they do condemn the gendered division of labour. Not only sexist incentives, but also sexist norms, are condemned. And, of course, it's likely that this is the kind of interpretation of the Basic Structure that Okin has in mind. But it's important to be clear what exactly it is that the principles condemn on this broader interpretation of the Basic Structure. To the extent that some unequal burden arises from natural differences between men and women, the division of labour is not condemned on either interpretation: for example, the fact that women, rather than men, bear children and lactate is not an injustice. Nor is every instance of unequal burden within a marriage, for example, objectionable. From the fact that some particular couple has divided the household labour so that the woman bears the greater burden of it, we cannot immediately conclude that a wrong has been done. Whereas the restricted interpretation of the Basic Structure allowed us to look only to the extent to which the coercive institutions influenced their decision, the expanded interpretation allows us to take into account that influence plus the influence of the ethos. That's it. To the extent to which those decisions are made whimsically, or to maximize the well-being of the family unit against a background in which there are no incentives or cultural norms pressing women generally to bear the greater burden, there is no injustice.

I want to finish by looking briefly at some comments on the relationship between justice as redistribution, which has been the focus of this book, and justice as recognition. Nancy Fraser argues that the tradition that focuses on the distribution of resources is one-sided, and that equally and independently important is the aspect of justice that has to do with whether people are properly 'recognized' as equals in society. Fraser has a full theory of justice, and although I shall not discuss it in detail, I do need to review it in order to bring out the significance of her comments about recognition.

Fraser's starting point, unlike that of all the theorists we have discussed up till now, is the real world. She identifies injustices in the real world, and tries to elaborate a theory which explains what is wrong with those injustices (why, that is, they are injustices) and guides us in what we would have to do to eliminate them. She starts by identifying maldistribution and misrecognition as distinctive wrongs. Maldistribution is the wrong that occurs when some person or group of people has fewer resources than justice requires or more resources than justice permits. Misrecognition is the wrong that occurs when some person or group of people is denied equal respect as a result of the 'institutionalized cultural patterns of interpretation and evaluation' prevailing in the society. Maldistribution is a consequence of the way the political economy is organized; misrecognition is a consequence of the way that the status order is designed.

Of course, maldistribution and misrecognition often come together. But they are conceptually distinct wrongs. African-Americans under Jim Crow laws were deprived both of resources and of respect, but each deprivation constituted a distinct injustice. They had, if you like, two quite separate grounds for complaint. It is entirely possible that members of some groups have only complaints of misrecognition, others only of maldistribution, and others still of both. So Fraser identifies two different kinds of group in society:

1 *Univalent collectivities* have their existences rooted solely in either the political economy or the status order, but not both (Fraser 1998: 11–12). Standard socialist accounts of the working class rooted its existence solely in the political economy, whereas accounts of gay and lesbian sexualities tend to see their existence (as a collectivity) as rooted in the status order. To say that a collectivity's existence is rooted in the status order, of course, is not to say that there are no common features among the people within the collectivity who compose it independently of the status order. Gay men are all gay, and they would all be gay even if homosexuality were not a despised sexuality. But they would not constitute a collectivity, any more

than tall men (who are all, indeed, tall) constitute a collectivity. Nor does the fact that a collectivity is univalent
mean that it only suffers one kind of wrong. Working-
class people may be misrecognized, and gay people may
be discriminated against economically so that they suffer
maldistribution. But the misrecognition suffered by a
group whose existence is rooted in the political economy
is a consequence of the maldistribution they suffer – solve
the problem of maldistribution, and the misrecognition
evaporates.

2   *Bivalent collectivities* have their existences rooted partly
in the political economy and partly in the status order.
Fraser's prime example of this is gender (Fraser 1998: 15).
Women, then, 'may suffer both socioeconomic maldistribution and cultural misrecognition in forms where neither
of these injustices is an indirect effect of the other, but
where both are primary and co-original' (Fraser 1998:
15). Bivalent collectivities, Fraser thinks, are in fact the
norm: even collectivities that appear to be univalent
usually, after investigation, turn out to be bivalent.

Fraser thinks that a theory of justice must give proper
weight to both these wrongs. Her theory is encapsulated in
what she calls the 'principle of participatory parity'. This
principle requires that social institutions be arranged so that
everyone can meet in public life as peers:

> It is unjust that some individuals and groups are denied the
> status of full partners in social interaction, simply as a con-
> sequence of institutionalized patterns of interpretation and
> evaluation in whose construction they have not equally par-
> ticipated and that disparage their distinctive characteristics or
> the distinctive characteristics assigned to them. (Fraser 1998:
> 24)

> Justice requires social arrangements that permit all (adult)
> members of society to interact with one another as peers.
> (Fraser 1998: 30)

Underlying this principle is the right to 'equal respect and/or
equal opportunity for achieving social esteem [which is a
necessary intersubjective condition for participatory parity]'

(Fraser 1998: 24). This right demands of social institutions that they be arranged to allow for participatory parity.

Fraser elaborates three conditions that would have to be met:

(a) formal legal equality: that is, there must be no legal discrimination against women, ethnic minorities, homosexuals, and so on (Fraser 1998: 30); in addition:
(b) 'the distribution of resources must be such as to ensure participants' independence and "voice"' (Fraser 1998: 30–1);
(c) 'Institutionalized cultural patterns of interpretation and evaluation express equal respect for all participants and ensure equal opportunity for achieving social esteem' (Fraser 1998: 31).

Fraser's theory has been taken up by left-leaning academics keen to draw on the resources of political theory to illuminate their sociological analyses and policy commentary (see, for example, Apple, Whitty, et al.). But the first two prongs of her theory of justice ((a) and (b) above) are very close to the views of traditional liberal egalitarian theorists. The third prong is the key to how Fraser's theory differs from standard liberal theories of justice, like Rawls's, Nussbaum's and even Nozick's. Fraser suggests that liberal egalitarians like Rawls wrongly reduce issues of recognition to issues of redistribution. But that seems wrong: if anything, the fundamental moral motivation for Rawls's theory is to ensure that social life is arranged so as to give proper recognition to people's status as free and equal persons. Nozick, Nussbaum, Friedman and Kymlicka, all in different ways, similarly seem to put recognition first. But the standard liberal view stops short of demanding that '[i]nstitutionalized cultural patterns of interpretation and evaluation express equal respect for all participants and ensure equal opportunity for achieving social esteem'. They concentrate, as Cohen points out, on the directly coercive legal structures, both because they think of the coercive character of social structures as standing in particularly urgent need of justification, and because they seek to justify their theories to adherents of a wide range of conflicting conceptions of the good.

Fraser has a particular problem, which Rawls and Nussbaum would also have if they were willing to endorse Fraser's third prong. She emphasizes that she is depending not on a sectarian conception of human flourishing, self-realization or the good, but on a theory of justice that 'can be accepted by those with divergent conceptions of the good' (Fraser 1998: 25). In particular, it does not depend for its force on the observation that oppression distorts the 'structure of self-consciousness of the oppressed' or derives from 'prejudice in the minds of the oppressors' (Fraser 1998: 26), and thus avoids victim-blaming and mind-policing. In other words she is aiming to provide a theory of justice that is 'political' in the sense that both Rawls and Nussbaum seek to provide 'political' liberal theories: it must be justifiable to a wide range of reasonable conceptions of the good.

But implementing the third prong would set the theory against many conceptions of the good that are, in fact, widely held in our societies. It is not just that many religious views consider homosexuality to be wrong, and prescribe sex-roles that systematically disadvantage women; it is also that many rationalistic conceptions of the good look down on religious belief and consider religious believers to be irrational in a substantial range of their reasoning. Schooling, and the public education of adults, would have simultaneously to combat these different kinds of attitudes. Put aside the thought that this would be difficult, in doing so the state would be setting itself against those very conceptions of the good within terms of which its theory of justice is supposed to be justifiable. Political theories always walk a fine line: they have to say enough to generate a theory of justice that makes distinctive demands about how social institutions are structured, but not so much that many reasonable conceptions of the good cannot be brought along.

Relatedly, implementing the third prong, at least in ways that went beyond altering the coercive legal structure, would also set Fraser against the principle of legitimacy elaborated earlier. Government intervention to manipulate the prevailing patterns of evaluation so that they conform with the government's evaluations, even when the government's evaluations are (objectively) right, will often contradict the principle of legitimacy, because it manufactures consent.

Conclusion

There is something intuitively right about the idea that the personal is political. Saying this allows us to account for the fact that it is not just coercive institutions but also less tangible and formal features of our common life (patterns of evaluation, cultural norms, the ethos) that influence how well our lives go, and that these matter when we are comparing different political options. But it does not require that we take the next step and assume that states are required to, or even permitted to, do whatever it takes to ensure justice. The personal, although political, is also still personal. There are stronger moral barriers against government intervention to shape the characters and motivations of individuals than against other forms of intervention to influence the distribution of resources and opportunities. To say this, though, is not to be quietistic, and in particular it does not force us to excuse those who use their advantaged position to exploit others, or even to seek their own even greater advantage when they could, instead, use it to benefit the least advantaged. We can quite well say that they are doing something wrong, which makes society less just, but which, perhaps regrettably, cannot rightly be prohibited.

9
Conclusion

I have surveyed a wide range of the perspectives found in contemporary theorizing about justice. I want to finish by indicating briefly some of the features that are common to most of the theories we have surveyed, and then offering some conservative thoughts about justice.

Common features

The theories of justice we have surveyed have three features in common. First, they are all critical theories. That is, they are theories which do not treat the political status quo as having intrinsic authority. The theories are arrived at by thinking about particular values, assessing how much and in what ways they matter, and establishing what broad institutional rules are implied by the proper ordering of values. They are not arrived at by looking at existing institutions and trying to establish what theoretical framework would justify them; they achieve a certain kind of critical distance, and ask us to evaluate existing institutions by reference to this distant standard. Of course, each theory endorses some aspects of some contemporary societies. Friedman's and Nozick's theories both endorse very roughly the basic rules of economic competition in contemporary capitalist societies, and Rawls's and Sen's theories support (in a very loose way) the broad outlines of redistributive taxation and the welfare state in some Western European countries. And all those theories, as well as Kymlicka's, offer (similar) justifications of the basic liberties guaranteed by most existing liberal democracies, although I would hazard that rigorous application of all those theories would require more secure guarantees of the liberties than most countries provide. Yet they are not meant to bolster any existing social order, but to provide an independent, rationally justifiable, basis for evaluating it.

Second, all the theories are individualistic in a certain sense: individuals are seen as the primary objects of moral concern, and corporate arrangements are justified by reference only to their likely effects on the quality of the lives of individuals. It is worth distinguishing this sense of individualism from some other senses. For example, none of the theories I have surveyed assumes or requires that individuals are normally or should be motivated entirely, or even mostly, by their own self-interested interests. All the theories are open to the possibility that altruism is both pervasive and a good thing. Indeed, defenders of the libertarian and classical liberal theories most frequently accused of being individualist in the wrong way sometimes argue that the limitations on redistribution that their theories require have the advantage of allowing more scope to altruistic impulses. Nor do they suggest that individuals are self-contained, self-reliant or 'asocial'. Rawls's assertion of the importance of developing a capacity for a sense of justice is a response to the fact that individuals have various moral interests that could not conceivably be developed outside of society. Indeed, humans cannot even learn to communicate without human society. They certainly cannot develop a sense of what it is to have a conception of the good life, or an active sense of justice, without social intercourse. All the theories we have looked at, in fact, assume this; the problem, for all theories, is how a social order should be regulated, given the assumption that human beings are intrinsically social beings.

I accept the weak form of individualism that these that theories share, but I should say that I find it hard to see how to argue for it, because it seems as obvious as anything that might be said in its favour. Consider one implication, which seems to me to support it. When we say that society has improved, we mean that society now better serves the interests of at least some of its members, or, possibly, some of its future members. For example, the shift toward a less sexist society has been a moral improvement only because it has meant that some individuals (many of them women) are genuinely better off than they were before. If you are an individualist in the sense that these theories share, and believe that the shift to a less sexist society has been a moral loss, it must be because you think that it has harmed individual people (and that this harm outweighs whatever benefits to individuals the change might have brought). But if individuals were not the primary objects of moral concern, it should be possible for society to have improved without there being anyone whose condition has improved from the moral point of view. We cannot prove that this could not be true, but the burden of proof is on the defender of such a claim.

The third feature most of the theories share is what is usually called anti-perfectionism. Anti-perfectionism is the view that the government should not require people to structure their lives according to a set of values that the government believes is true and worthy, *even if the government is right to believe them true and worthy*. All of the views we have looked at, including Margalit and Halbertal's, set sharp constraints on the extent to which the government is entitled to coerce people for their own good. Anti-perfectionism is, though, a matter of degree. All the theories incorporate some reference to moral values which, by implication, guide government action. So, for example, Rawls's theory has the three fundamental intuitive ideas – all of which are moral ideas – at its foundation, and in particular says that human beings have a higher-order interest in being able to exercise and develop their capacities for a sense of justice and conception of the good. Friedman asserts the importance of managing one's own life according to one's own judgements and values – which he thinks of as something which contributes enormously to human flourishing. Nozick's side-constraints depend for their appeal on the idea that it is good for people to be able to control their own lives. So whereas all the theories are anti-perfectionist, none of them completely disavows controversial moral judgements about the good. But they do all restrain the government from imposing a single comprehensive way of life on its citizens, and also refrain from invoking such a theory in justifying the principles of justice they assert.

In modern liberal democracies moderate anti-perfection-ism seems obviously right. But that is a relatively new phenomenon: many human societies have adopted fairly restrictive social norms, and even today in many parts of the world there are strong movements to base social institutions on comprehensive views about how to live one's life that would be controversial in those societies if there were suffi-cient protections for freedom of expression and freedom of conscience that dissent could be openly expressed. Most Western European countries have spent several hundred of the past thousand years under social institutions justified by reference to one or another version of Christianity, and several countries in the Middle East today justify their social institutions by reference to some version of Islam. These insti-tutions are perfectionist in the relevant sense. But even moderate anti-perfectionists will disagree amongst themselves about what moral values should be allowed to play a justifi-catory role. And it is possible that some anti-perfectionists underestimate the extent to which perfectionist values might be needed to justify certain of our institutions that they would not want to criticize as unjust. Consider marriage, for example. Why should the state privilege a particular con-tractual arrangement in people's essentially personal lives, to the extent that it enters that contract as a party and restricts various benefits only to people who enter that arrangement? Most of the social benefits of the arrangement and the bene-fits to children could be achieved without there being a special, privileged, arrangement and instead by allowing people to contract with each other as they choose. The dis-tinctive benefit of privileging a particular marriage contract is that it prompts people to consider making long-term com-mitments, and publicizing them so that they are more diffi-cult to dissolve. If the state is justified in doing this, it must be because it brings some good to the parties to the rela-tionship that would otherwise be more elusive. Here's a pos-sible argument: human beings have a systematic tendency to live for the day. This inclines them to engage in relationships, especially intimate and sexual relationships, on a short-term and temporary basis. If these relationships last, it is often because of inertia rather than commitment. But intimate relationships are more rewarding, and are more carefully entered into, when they are lasting relationships, and where the lastingness is a result of commitment, so that they involve negotiation over long-term plans. However, since each of us has only one life, we are not able to learn this from experience until, for many of us, it is too late. So the government is justified in providing people with incentives to make long-term commitments in their intimate relationships, and, perhaps more importantly, in prompting them to decide whether or not to make the relevant commitments. A privileged marriage contract achieves this goal. It does not, of course, force people into commitments, so it is mildly perfectionistic – it allows people to make their own judgements and live by them. But the justification does invoke a claim about what makes for human flourishing, and one that is liable to be controversial among reasonable people.

Some conservative thoughts

Observant readers will notice that I have not included in the book any theories of justice that would count as conservative. This may reflect a bias in the author, but I don't think so. My aim has been to provide a fair view of the current state of the contemporary debate about theories of justice. I think it is fair to say that there just isn't a contemporary theory of justice that properly qualifies as conservative. Some readers might think of Friedman, and others, perhaps, of Nozick, as conservatives, but I do not think that is fair – they both believe that social institutions have to be justified rationally, and neither of them accords any fundamental authority to the status quo. That there are no contemporary conservative theories of justice in the debate should not be taken to mean that there are no contemporary conservative theorists or perspectives in the debate; and, in fact, the communitarian critique of justice which inspires the group-rights views surveyed in chapter 6 is basically a conservative critique. I want to conclude the book by raising some conservative thoughts and explaining why they might matter in thinking about justice.

The first conservative thought is analogous to a thought that many readers have had when managers at their workplaces propose changes in their working environments. If you were to review the basic managerial structure of any firm, school, university or household, it would be astonishing if you found that those structures were perfectly efficient. They have evolved in response to internal power struggles and changing external conditions; and the current situation almost certainly contains different internal power relations and different external incentives from those in response to which the institution has evolved. So, when a new manager takes over, or a management consultant is brought in to make a strategic review, she will almost certainly find that it would be more efficient for the firm to be organized differently. Let's suppose she proposes a set of reforms that, on paper, seems more efficient. Workers will often have two responses. The first is this: look, we can see these reforms might lead to a more efficient workplace. But implementing them will be very costly, and will take time, and by the time they are adopted we may be no better off than we are with the current arrangements. The second is this: we can see the benefits of these reforms, because those are the effects that you have thought through and highlighted. But they will probably have effects that we cannot anticipate right now, and some of *those* effects will be negative. The probability of bad unintended consequences makes us sceptical of the reforms.

Conservatives can similarly acknowledge the imperfection of existing arrangements but defend them against many purported moral improvements. Institutional reforms always intrinsically impose costs on some people (for example, increasing the marginal tax rate imposes costs on taxpayers). But there are also, almost always, extrinsic costs: the costs of allaying opposition and overcoming resistance, which are greater the stronger the opposition and resistance. And the benefits are never certain: proponents of a reform can usually demonstrate that it will have some discrete benefit, but they cannot, almost by definition, meet the objection that their proposal will almost certainly have unintended consequences.

The larger the scale of the reform, the more vulnerable it is to this sort of objection. And all of the theories we have surveyed would require large-scale reform for full implementation.

I do not mean to endorse this conservative thought unconditionally. But it does at least, I think, support a mild conservative bias in our thinking about justice and reform. Theorists of justice are entitled to endorse radical principles of justice, as long as those principles are feasible in the sense discussed in chapter 2. But it is incumbent on reformers motivated by an ideal of social justice to think through the intrinsic and extrinsic transition costs, and also to acknowledge the reality of unintended consequences when proposing a reform. Some injustices are sufficiently bad, and some reforms sufficiently mild, that this conservative thought has very little bearing on the issue. But where an unjustice is mild, or a reform ambitious, the conservative thought imposes a burden of proof on the reformer.

A second conservative thought is that the value of justice is often overestimated by theorists of justice. Justice matters, certainly, and some conservatives accept the broad strokes of Friedman's view; some even accept variants of Rawls's. But they can dispute that justice is, to use Rawls's phrase, 'the first virtue of social institutions' or dispute that being the first virtue makes it as important as theorists like Rawls and Nozick treat it as being. There are other good things as well as justice, and other bad things as well as injustice. Various human excellences matter – the art produced by the great artist; the comradeship and courage brought forth by the experience of battle; the love, intimacy and self-sacrifice realized in the best family relationships – and sometimes these goods may compete with justice. Again, conservatives do not need to reject any particular theory of justice, but they can resist efforts to implement it on the grounds that such efforts may bring about the loss of other, vital, human goods. This concern is articulately presented in an argument Michael Sandel makes in the course of a lengthy critique of Rawls's theory (but which could be applied to any of the theorists I have looked at so far): 'to invoke the circumstances of justice is simultaneously to concede, implicitly at least, the circumstances of benevolence, or fraternity, or of enlarged affections' (Sandel 1981: 32). Sandel argues by analogy with the family, which is an institution where these alternative circumstances hold, and where they would be driven out by the primacy of justice:

> Consider, for example, the more or less ideal family situation, where relations are governed in large part by spontaneous affection and where, in consequence, the circumstances of justice prevail to a relatively small degree. Individual rights and fair decision procedures are seldom invoked, not because injustice is rampant but because their appeal is pre-empted by a spirit of generosity in which I am rarely inclined to claim my fair share. . . . Now imagine that one day the harmonious family comes to be wrought with dissension. Interests grow divergent and the circumstances of justice grow more acute . . . affection and spontaneity . . . gives way to demands of fairness and observance of rights . . . the old generosity is replaced by a judicious temper of unexceptionable integrity and the new moral necessities are met with a full measure of justice. . . . Are we to say that the arrival of justice, however full, restores the full moral character and the only difference is a psychological one? (Sandel 1981: 33)

The answer, of course, to the rhetorical question, is 'no'. The view is that justice drives out beneficence; it is the enemy of the enlarged affections within the family. So Rawls, and other liberals, are wrong to focus on justice as the first virtue of institutions; it is, at best, one among many, potentially competing, goods. Now, there are reasons to be wary of analogies with the family, and also of the claim that justice drives out affection within the family. Justice does not require that people always claim what is due to them: there is nothing unjust when, as often happens in affectionate families, loving siblings or parents waive what is due to them for the sake of their sibling or child. But what if there were good reasons for believing that justice competed with other goods in society? It would be excessive to say that justice was so valuable that it should be fully implemented even if in doing so we wiped out much of what makes life worth living.

Of course, conservatives who make this kind of argument in public debate rarely concede that they are arguing for injustice; they prefer to adopt, at least publicly, rhetoric about justice that is congruent with the availability of the goods they want to protect. But my point is that they *could* concede that the arrangement they prefer is unjust, and still have a reasonable point. Again, if implementing justice deprived us of many of those things that made life worth living, that would count, somewhat, against implementing justice. It would not be a vindication of simply any injustice, of course, even of those injustices required, say, to maximize the availability of the human good. Justice matters, and one of the reasons injustice is bad is that it unfairly deprives some people of access to vitally important human goods. I should emphasize that I am generally sceptical of claims that justice inhibits the availability of vital human goods, which is one reason why I am not a conservative. But such claims are not obviously false; they have to be considered on a case-by-case basis, and when there is some truth in them the theorist of justice is obliged to make accommodations.

A final conservative thought is the complement to the second. Some conservatives believe that human beings are pervasively prone to evil, and that implementing some of the theories of justice I have surveyed, while it might be, in some sense, 'fair', would give greater scope to evil than institutions that gave less sway to individual conscience and personal liberty. The purpose of government, on this view, is to restrain human beings from doing evil to each other, regardless of whether or not the measures required for this purpose are fair. John Kekes is a contemporary conservative thinker who exemplifies this thought. Evil is, according to Kekes, 'unjustified . . . harm which must be serious enough to damage its victim's capacity to function normally' (Kekes 1998: 26). Kekes suggests that evil is not merely a contingent response in humans to the flawed social institutions in which they find themselves. Evil is, rather, deep in human nature: a feature of the human condition to which institutional design must respond, rather than one which institutions cause. He also thinks that a vast number of people are either evildoers or potential evildoers. He says,

> If evil is prevalent, evildoers must be numerous. It is to be
> expected then that in a liberal society there will be a moral
> minority whose actions are morally acceptable and for whom

autonomy, freedom, equality, rights, pluralism and distributive justice are guaranteed, while the remaining immoral majority, to whose actions the prevalence of evil is due, will have their conduct curbed . . . if evil is prevalent there seems to be no reasonable alternative. (Kekes 1998: 42)

Now, Kekes is not necessarily right that the pervasiveness of evil in human society is necessarily evidence that a majority of people are evildoers. As any organizer of a terrorist cell knows, a very few people can do a great deal of evil to a great number of people. If the evidence in the trial of Timothy McVeigh is to be believed, it took just two evildoers and a truck full of fertilizer to destroy 151 lives and wreak havoc on many hundreds more. The Holocaust required the active participation of many Europeans, and the acquiescence of many more, but it is not at all clear that anything close to a majority of Europeans (or even Germans) participated malevolently in this contender for the greatest of all human evils.

But suppose that Kekes's pessimistic outlook were correct. What would this mean for justice as it is conceived by Rawls et al.? The answer to that question depends, I think, on whether we think that institutions which better embody justice make evil more or less likely. Again, I tend to think that more just institutions in fact tend to reduce the scope for evildoing. I think we have evidence that institutions in which citizens are more rather than less equal and more rather than less free produce less evil than do institutions which restrict individual freedoms and instantiate hierarchies of inequality. This may be because such institutions better enable the potential victims of evil to protect themselves against evil, and thereby to deter evildoers. So, again, I don't believe that the conservative thought we are considering really counts against justice. But I do think there is a rational kernel to the thought, which is that evil is bad, and since we cannot show by conceptual argument that justice crowds out evil, we have to be open to the possibility that there are, sometimes, trade-offs between increasing justice and diminishing evil; and that when these trade-offs present themselves, it will sometimes be right to decide in favour of injustice, and against evil.

Notes

Chapter 3 John Rawls's Theory of Justice as Fairness

1 Rawls died in 2002.

Chapter 4 The Capability Approach

1 In his own discussion Sen actually presents this consideration as an objection to utilitarianism. Utilitarianism says that we should act so as to maximize average preference satisfaction, so it implies that violating one person's rights is justified, even if they do mind, if doing so satisfies enough of other people's preferences. But even if, instead of calling for maximizing average preference satisfaction, we called for equalizing preference satisfaction, that view could not grant the special status to rights that they intuitively have, which is why I have presented the argument as one against the preference satisfaction metric, rather than against thoroughgoing utilitarianism.
2 See Barry (in press: chap. 17) for an elaboration of this point.
3 I'm grateful to Judith Suissa for clarifying these points to me.

Chapter 5 Libertarian Justice

1 If, like me, you find implausible the assumption that basketball could be entertaining, substitute an alternative, entertaining, sport.

Chapter 6 Justice and Groups

1   See also Kymlicka (1995: 109), where he says:

> The viability of their [national minorities'] societal cul-
> tures may be undermined by economic and political deci-
> sions made by the majority. They could be outbid or
> outvoted on resources and policies that are crucial to the
> survival of their societal cultures. The members of the
> majority do not face this problem. Given the importance
> of cultural membership this is a significant inequality
> which, if not addressed, becomes a serious injustice.

2   There is, in fact, a well-known Welsh popular group called the
    Super Furry Animals which self-consciously produces occasional
    Welsh-language albums. These are not its most popular albums.
3   See Sterba (1996) for a concise, if shocking, account of some of
    these wrongs.
4   For Dworkin's version of the initial auction, see Dworkin
    (1981).
5   For a less formal rendering of the main argument I am discussing
    here, see Kymlicka (1995: 108–15).
6   There are, presumably, some people who lack a cultural context
    of choice: for example, most obviously, feral children (children
    who are raised in the wild). But it is not clear that anything can
    be done about this except searching for them and placing them
    in societies.

Chapter 7 Affirmative Action, Equality of Opportunity and the Gendered Division of Labour

1   'Female Genital Mutilation: Is it Crime or Culture?', *The Econo-
    mist*, 13 February 1999. For further discussion of female genital
    mutilation, and a detailed refutation of attempts to justify tol-
    eration of the practice, see Nussbaum (1998: ch. 4).

A Guide to Further Reading

This book is intended to be read alongside the literature it discusses. I've deliberately focused on a small number of books and essays, because I believe the detail of the positions is important (and this is a short book). I've chosen the literature because it represents what I regard as the most important perspectives on justice in the contemporary debates.

However, the book taken alone, or even in combination with the literature it is about, may give the false impression that abstract theory is most of what goes on in contemporary debates about justice. Far from it. There is a wealth of literature on contemporary moral and political issues that both applies lessons learned from theorizing about justice, and draws on those issues to make further theoretical progress. I have organized the recommendations below into two categories: the first contains work that engages directly with the literature discussed here; the second contains work about contemporary issues that engages with or draws on this literature.

Theories

The best scholarly source on Rawls is now Samuel Freeman's edited collection *The Cambridge Companion to Rawls* (Cambridge University Press, 2003), which contains an extensive and well-organized bibliography on Rawls. Also well worth reading, if you can find it, is Thomas Pogge's book *Realizing Rawls* (Columbia University Press, 1989). Other crucial literature on liberalism includes Joseph Raz, *The Morality of Freedom* (Oxford University Press, 1986) and Ronald Dworkin, *A Matter of Principle* (Harvard University Press, 1985). On the capability approach there is a wealth of literature. Sabine Alkire's *Valuing Freedoms* (Oxford University Press, 2002) is the place to start. Loren Lomasky's *Persons, Rights, and the Moral Community* (Oxford University Press, 1987) is an excellent attempt to justify a moderate libertarianism. Will Kymlicka, in addition to the monographs I discuss, has an excellent edited collection of articles on the debate about group rights called *The Rights of Minority Cultures* (Oxford University Press, 1985). Interested readers should also read Brian Barry's extended argument against group-based perspectives, *Culture and Equality* (Polity, 2001).

Issues

I have restricted myself to recommending *books* on particular issues. All of these books contain a combination of philosophical theorizing about justice and applications to particular cases. The titles should make it obvious which topic they address.

Archard, David, *Children, Family, and the State* (Ashgate Publishing, 2003)

Archard, David and Colin MacLeod (eds) *The Moral and Political Status of Children* (Oxford University Press, 2002)

Baird, Robert and Stuart Rosenbaum (eds) *The Ethics of Abortion: Pro-Choice Versus Pro-Life* (Prometheus Books, 1993)

Buchanan, Allen, Dan Brock, Norman Daniels and Daniel Wikler, *From Chance to Choice* (Cambridge University Press, 2000)

Cahn, Stephen (ed.) *The Affirmative Action Debates* (Routledge, 2002)

Daniels, Norman, *Just Health Care* (Cambridge University Press, 1985)

Kamm, Frances Myrna, *Creation and Abortion* (Oxford University Press, 1992)

Kittay, Eva Feder, *Love's Labor: Essays on Women, Equality, and Dependency* (Routledge 1999)

Moellendorf, Darrel, *Cosmopolitan Justice* (Westview Press, 2000)

Pogge, Thomas, *World Poverty and Human Rights* (Polity, 2002)

Walzer, Michael, *Just and Unjust Wars* (Basic Books, 1977)

Bibliography

Barry, Brian (in press) *Why Social Justice Matters* (Polity)

Buchanan, Allen (1997) 'Theories of Secession', *Philosophy and Public Affairs*, 26, 31–61

Buchanan, Allen, Daniel Brock, Norman Daniels and Daniel Wikler (2000) *From Chance to Choice* (Cambridge University Press)

Cohen, G.A. (1997) 'Where the Action Is: On the Site of Distributive Justice', *Philosophy and Public Affairs*, 26, 3–30

Cohen, Joshua (1993) 'Freedom of Expression', *Philosophy and Public Affairs*, 22, 207–63

Daniels, Norman (1985) *Just Health Care* (Cambridge University Press)

Dworkin, Ronald (1981) 'What is Equality? Part 2: Equality of Resources', *Philosophy and Public Affairs*, 10, 283–345

Fraser, Nancy (1998) 'Social Justice in the Age of Identity Politics' *The Tanner Lectures on Human Values* at *http://www.tannerlectures.utah.edu/lectures/Fraser98.pdf*

Friedman, Milton (1962) *Capitalism and Freedom* (University of Chicago Press)

Galston, William (2002) *Liberal Pluralism* (Cambridge University Press)

Hayek, Friedrich (1960) *The Constitution of Liberty* (University of Chicago Press)

Hochschild, Arlie (1989) *The Second Shift* (Viking)

Kant, Immanuel (1998) *Groundwork of the Metaphysics of Morals*, ed. Mary Gregor (Cambridge University Press)

Kekes, John (1998) *Against Liberalism* (Cornell University Press)

Kymlicka, Will (1989) *Liberalism, Community and Culture* (Oxford University Press)

Kymlicka, Will (1995) *Multicultural Citizenship* (Oxford University Press)

Langton, Rae (1993) 'Speech Acts and Unspeakable Acts', *Philosophy and Public Affairs*, 22, 305–30

Lenin, V.I. (1964) 'How to Guarantee the Success of the Constituent Assembly', in *Collected Works*, Vol. 25 (Progress Publishers)

Levine, Andrew (1999) 'Rewarding Effort', *Journal of Political Philosophy*, 7, 404–18

Margalit, Avishai and Moshe Halbertal (1994) 'Liberalism and the Right to Culture', *Social Research*, 61, 491–510

Miller, David (1995) *On Nationality* (Oxford University Press)

Moellendorf, Darrel (2000) *Cosmopolitan Justice* (Westview Press)

Nozick, Robert (1974) *Anarchy, State and Utopia* (Basic Books)

Nussbaum, Martha (1998) *Sex and Social Justice* (Oxford University Press)

Nussbaum, Martha (2000) *Women and Human Development* (Cambridge University Press)

Okin, Susan Moller (1987) 'Justice and Gender', *Philosophy and Public Affairs*, 16, 42–72

Okin, Susan Moller (1999) *Is Multiculturalism Bad for Women?* (Princeton University Press)

Rawls, John (1971) *A Theory of Justice* (Harvard University Press)

Rawls, John (1980) 'Kantian Constructivism in Moral Theory', *Journal of Philosophy*, 77, 515–72

Rawls, John (1992) *Political Liberalism* (Columbia University Press)

Rawls, John (1999) *A Theory of Justice* (revised edn) (Harvard University Press)

Rawls, John (2001) *Justice as Fairness* (Harvard University Press)

Sandel, Michael (1981) *Liberalism and the Limits of Justice* (Cambridge University Press)

Scanlon T.M. (1972) 'A Theory of Freedom of Expression', *Philosophy and Public Affairs*, 1, 204–26

Sen, Amartya (1999) *Development as Freedom* (Knopf)

Sterba, James P. (1996) 'Understanding Evil: American Slavery, the Holocaust, and the Conquest of the American Indians', *Ethics*, 106, 424–48.

Swift, Adam (2001) *Political Philosophy: An Introduction for Politicians and Undergraduates* (Polity)

Swift, Adam (2003) *How Not to be a Hypocrite: School Choice for the Morally Perplexed Parent* (RoutledgeFalmer).

Swift, Adam (in press) 'Justice, Luck and the Family' in Samuel Bowles, Herbert Gintis and Melissa Osborne (eds) *Unequal Chances* (Princeton University Press)

Thomson, Judith (1971) 'A Defense of Abortion', *Philosophy and Public Affairs*, 1, 47–66

Walzer, Michael (1977) *Just and Unjust Wars* (Basic Books)

Weithman, Paul (2000) *Religion and the Obligations of Citizenship* (Cambridge University Press)

Wilkinson, Richard (1996) *Unhealthy Societies* (Routledge)

Williams, Andrew (1998) 'Incentives, Inequality, and Publicity', *Philosophy and Public Affairs*, 27, 225–47

World Bank (2001) *Engendering Development Through Gender Equality in Rights, Resources and Voice* (Oxford University Press)

Index